OMG!
GALLERY
BOOKS
XXX

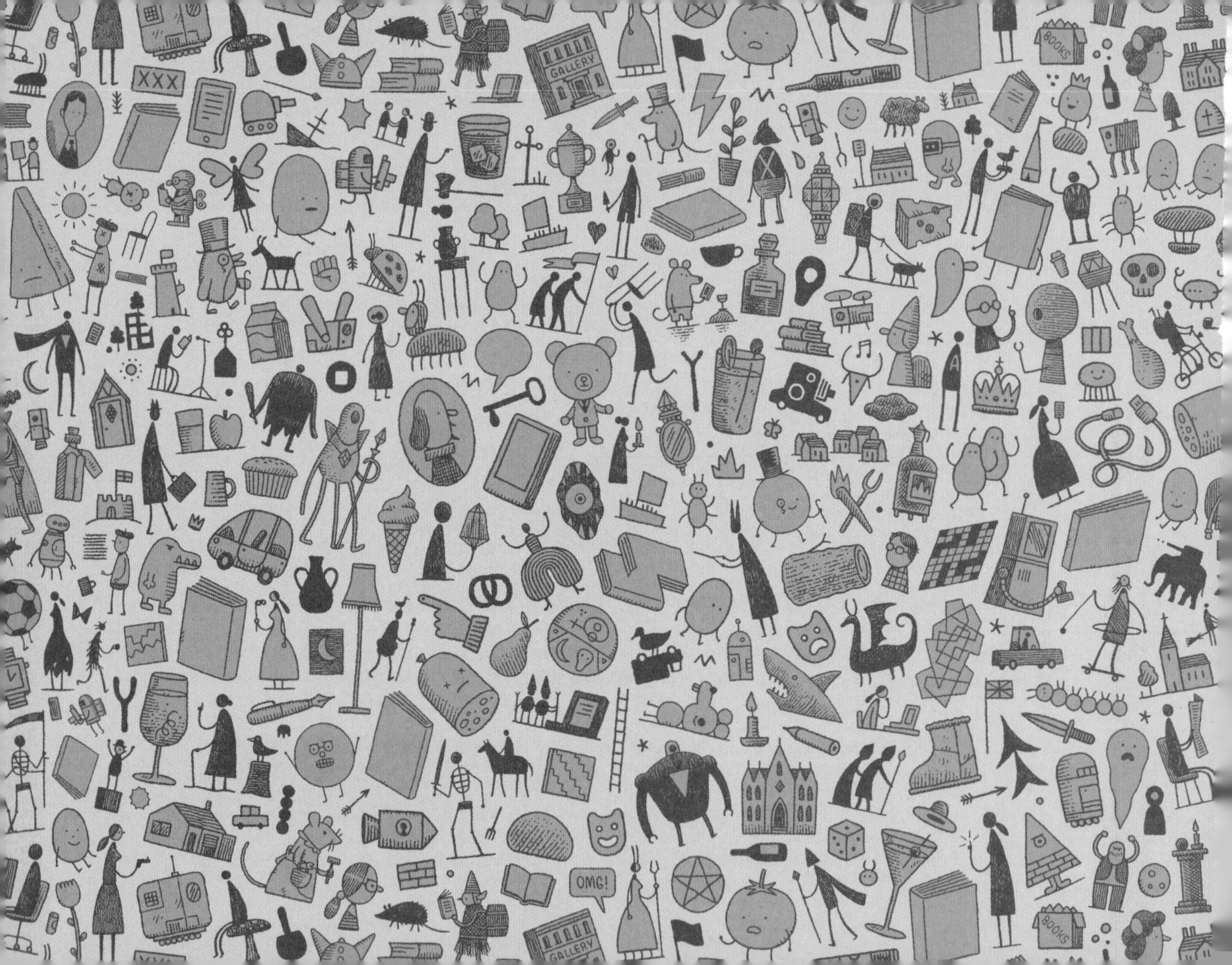
XXX
GALLERY
BOOKS
OMG!

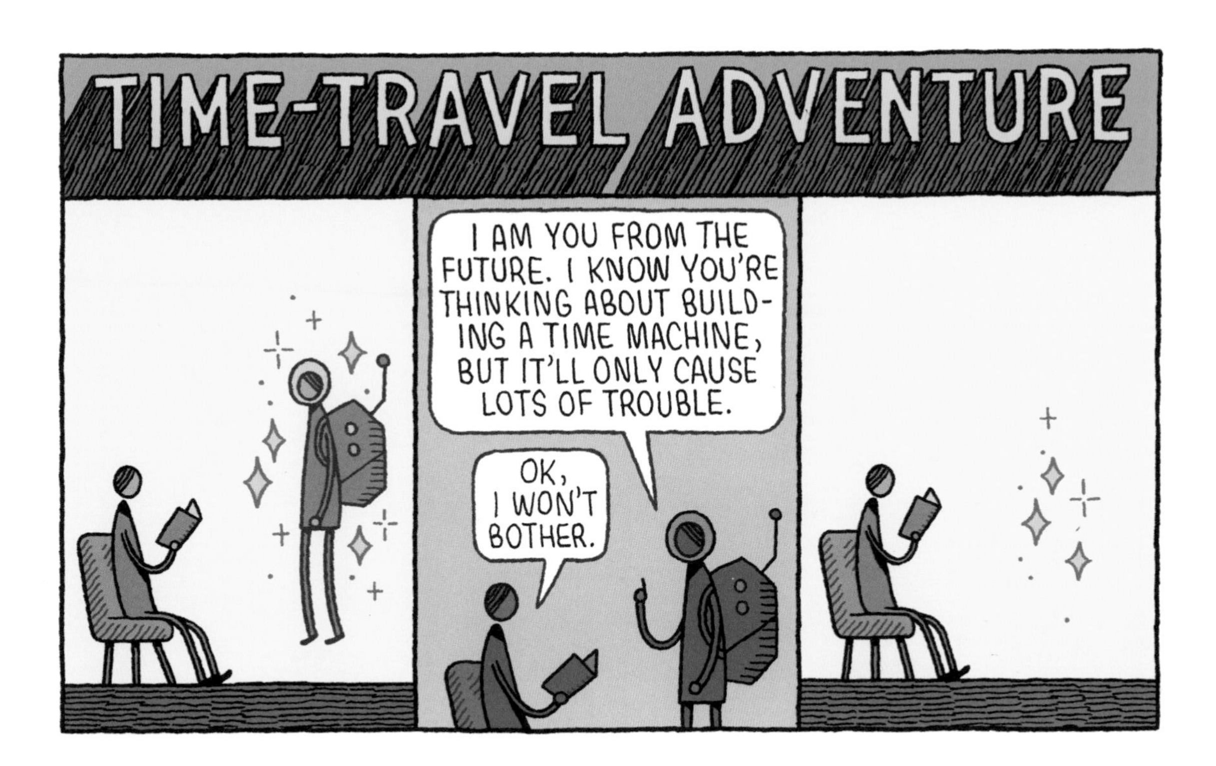
TIME-TRAVEL ADVENTURE
I AM YOU FROM THE FUTURE. I KNOW YOU'RE THINKING ABOUT BUILD-ING A TIME MACHINE, BUT IT'LL ONLY CAUSE LOTS OF TROUBLE.
OK, I WON'T BOTHER.

FIRST HARDCOVER EDITION: OCTOBER 2017
SECOND HARDCOVER PRINTING: JANUARY 2018
PRINTED IN CHINA
10 9 8 7 6 5 4 3 2

LIBRARY AND ARCHIVES CANADA
CATALOGUING IN PUBLICATION

GAULD, TOM
BAKING WITH KAFKA / COMICS BY TOM GAULD

ISBN 978-1-77046-296-0 (HARDCOVER)

1. COMICS (GRAPHIC WORKS) I. TITLE

PN6737.G38B38 2017 741.5'69411 C2017-901679-2

DISTRIBUTED IN THE USA BY:
FARRAR, STRAUS AND GIROUX
ORDERS: 888.330.8477

DISTRIBUTED IN CANADA BY:
RAINCOAST BOOKS
ORDERS: 800.663.5714

BAKING WITH KAFKA

COMICS BY
TOM GAULD

DRAWN & QUARTERLY

FOR DAPHNE AND IRIS

OUR DEAR, DEPARTED BOOKS...
DROPPED IN THE BATH
LENT TO AN UNRELIABLE FRIEND
ACCIDENTALLY RECYCLED WITH THE NEWSPAPERS
LEFT ON A BUS
MAULED BY A BABY
TAKEN ON AN ITALIAN HOLIDAY AND NEVER CAME BACK
MIGHT BE IN ONE OF THOSE BOXES IN THE BASEMENT

THE SET TEXT

HELLO THERE!
I'M SO EXCITED THAT YOU'RE GOING TO BE STUDYING ME THIS TERM!
WE'RE GOING TO HAVE A GREAT TIME!!
LOOKING ME UP ON WIKIPEDIA: WHAT A GREAT IDEA! IT CAN BE USEFUL TO GET SOME CONTEXT BEFORE READING A NOVEL.
DOWNLOADING THE MOVIE ADAPTATION: EXCELLENT!
YOU'LL LOVE WATCHING IT AFTER YOU'VE READ ME!
OR BEFORE!
THAT'S FINE, TOTALLY FINE!
AH, I SEE!
YOU'RE WRITING THE ESSAY NOW SO THAT YOU CAN FOCUS COMPLETELY ON READING LATER!
IT'S GOING TO BE SUCH FUN!!

ARABELLA!! A LETTER FOR YOU FROM MISTER HASTINGS!
OH MY!! READ IT TO ME AT ONCE!

"MADAM, IT WAS MY SINCEREST PLEASURE TO MEET YOU AT THE HEATHRIDGE BALL. I TRUST YOU WILL NOT THINK ME FORWARD IN EXPRESSING MY HOPE THAT WE MAY RENEW OUR ACQUAINTANCE AT THE FIRST OPPORTUNITY. SMILEY FACE. HEART. SMILEY FACE WITH HEARTS FOR EYES. THUMBS UP. FLOWER. SMILEY FACE BLOWING A KISS. HEART."

SOME MURDER METHODS FOR MODERN MYSTERY WRITERS
POISONED ARTISANAL BRIOCHE
RUN OVER BY SELF-DRIVING CAR
ORGANIC, LOCALLY-SOURCED CYANIDE
EXPLODING E-CIGARETTE
STRANGLED WITH SMARTPHONE CHARGER CABLE
BLUDGEONED WITH SUSTAINABLE FIREWOOD
SCORPION HIDDEN IN UGGS
PUSHED OFF CLIFF WHILE INSTAGRAMMING

2014
RE-INTRODUCING THE FAIRY TO OUR COUNTRYSIDE WILL IMPROVE THE FAILING ECOSYSTEM.
2017
THE ONLY WAY TO DEAL WITH OUR FAIRY INFESTATION IS TO BRING BACK THEIR NATURAL PREDATOR: TROLLS.
2020
TROLL NUMBERS ARE OUT OF CONTROL. WE NEED DRAGONS TO PREY ON THEM.
2023
SOMETHING MUST BE DONE ABOUT OUR DRAGON PROBLEM. I'M THINKING GIANT ROBOTIC SPIDERS, AN ARMY OF SKELETONS OR GODZILLA.

THE FOUR UNDRAMATIC PLOT STRUCTURES

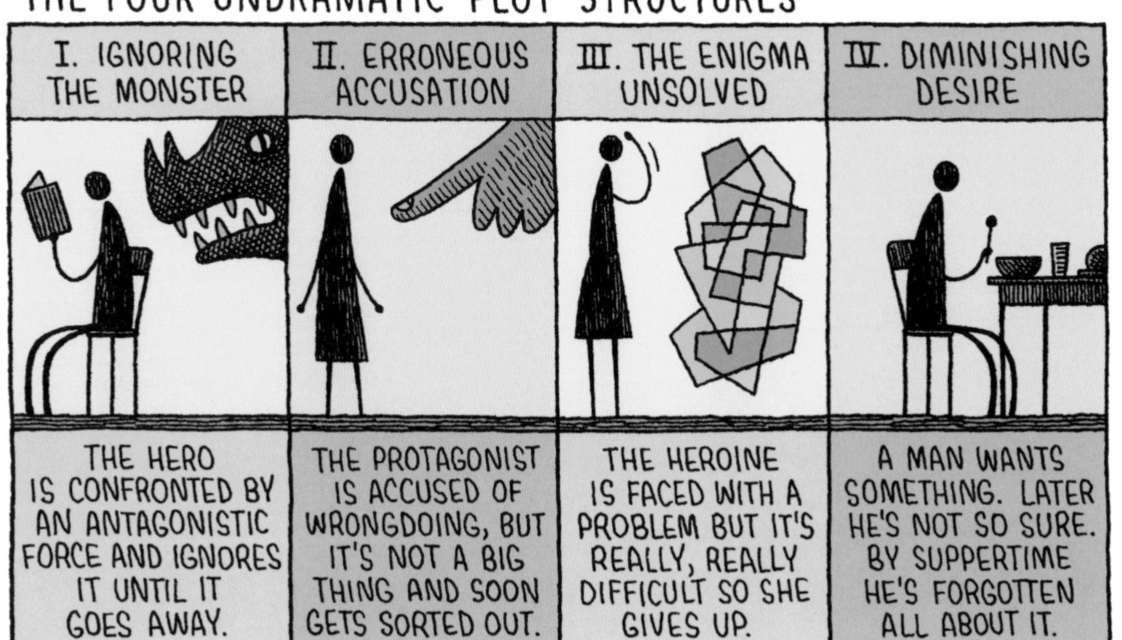

REVOLUTION!
FRIENDS! WE MUST SMASH THE WHOLE SYSTEM AND BEGIN SOCIETY ANEW!
BOO
MADNESS!
COUNT ME OUT
OK...WE NEED TO BRING DOWN THE GOVERNMENT!
NO THANKS
CHAOS!
OH DEAR
WE COULD MARCH ON PARLIAMENT AND DEMAND CHANGE?
HMM...
MAYBE
NOT SURE
-SIGH- WOULD ANYONE LIKE TO SIGN A PETITION?
PASS THE PEN!
THAT'S MORE LIKE IT!
POWER TO THE PEOPLE!

Scenes from 'Mrs Tittlemouse joins the Suffragettes' by Beatrix Potter

"We must fight for our freedoms and those of our daughters." Mrs Tittlemouse explained to the ladybird.

"The inferiority of women is a hideous lie which has been enforced by law." she told the fat old toad.

"Deeds not words." said Mrs Tittlemouse and went off to town to smash windows with her toffee hammer.

MY LIBRARY

READ.
INTENDING TO READ.
HALF-READ.
PRETEND I'VE READ.
SAVING FOR WHEN I HAVE MORE TIME.
WILL NEVER READ.
PURELY FOR SHOW.
READ, BUT CAN'T REMEMBER A SINGLE THING ABOUT IT.
WISH I HADN'T READ.

BEWARE!
X
TH' POEMS HEREWITH ART MOST TERRIBLY BAWDY.
CLICK HITHER TO CONFIRME THY AGE:
I AM AG'D SIXTEENE OR OVER

OUR BLESSED HOMELAND
THEIR BARBAROUS WASTES
OUR GLORIOUS LEADER
OUR GREAT RELIGION
OUR NOBLE POPULACE
OUR HEROIC ADVENTURERS
THEIR BRUTISH INVADERS
THEIR BACKWARD SAVAGES
THEIR PRIMITIVE SUPERSTITION
THEIR WICKED DESPOT

MY NEW NOVEL IS AVAILABLE IN THE FOLLOWING FORMATS
BOOK
AUDIOBOOK
E-BOOK
DRONE-BOOK
NANOBOOK
HOLOGRAPHIC INFORMATION CRYSTAL
RECITED BY A MECHANICAL RAVEN
ODOURLESS GAS
EXPLAINED BY A PATRONISING ROBOT
T-SHIRT

YOU MUST TAKE THE ENCHANTED BLADE TO THE DRAGON-KING OF MOUNT IZHKA'HAR. ONLY HE CAN SAVE US FROM THE DEMON-FIRESTORM!
HOW DO I GET TO MOUNT IZHKA'HAR?
I'VE CREATED A QUEST.APP ROUTE AND SHARED IT WITH YOU.
I DON'T SEE IT.
LOOK IN YOUR 'NEW QUESTS' FOLDER.
IT'S NOT THERE.
HAVE YOU GOT 'SYNCH ROUTES' TURNED ON?
YES. TRY TAGGING ME AS A 'TRUSTED COMPANION'.
IT'S NOT LETTING ME!
I'LL LOOK IN THE MANUAL...
"TO CREATE A MULTI-USER ROUTE YOU MUST UPGRADE TO QUEST.APP PRO."
#✪@*!

THE HILLS
HEY, FRANK.
WHAT?
NEVER MIND, YOU HAD SOMETHING ON YOUR HEAD, BUT IT'S GONE NOW.

Keyboard Shortcuts for Novelists

[↑] [/] [H] FIND AND FILL PLOT HOLES

[←] [P] [.] MAKE PROTAGONIST MORE LIKEABLE

[B] [–] [ctrl] REMOVE BORING BITS

[alt] [F2] INSERT CHARACTER:

+ [\] [B] SAGE BARTENDER
+ []] [D] TALKING DOG
+ [,] [L] LONG-LOST SIBLING

[cmd] [alt] ADD:

+ [3] [2] SEXUAL TENSION
+ [4] [9] PLOT TWIST
+ [7] [8] HUMOROUS INTERLUDE

[↑] [=] CHANGE SETTING TO:

+ [F6] [T] TUDOR ENGLAND
+ [F4] [L] WWII LIFEBOAT
+ [F3] [J] JUPITER, 2250

THE ANGRY MOB
BOILING WITH RAGE
VERY ANGRY
ANGRY BUT NOT SURE WHY
A TINY BIT ANGRY
NOT SURE
PRETENDING TO BE ANGRY
JUST LIKES BEING IN A MOB

BAKING WITH KAFKA
THIS WEEK
LEMON DRIZZLE CAKE

I HAVE THE TRUE FEELING OF MYSELF ONLY WHEN I AM UNBEARABLY UNHAPPY.

TO DIE WOULD SIMPLY BE TO SURRENDER A NOTHING TO THE NOTHING.

THE MEANING OF LIFE IS THAT IT STOPS.
NEXT WEEK
BANOFFEE PIE!

TOWN MOUSE

I SHALL PAY A VISIT TO COUNTRY MOUSE. HIS BACKWARD WAYS NEVER FAIL TO MAKE ME FEEL BETTER ABOUT MYSELF.
HELLO, HIPSTER MOUSE. WHAT ARE YOU DOING HERE?
I'M AIRBNB-ING COUNTRY MOUSE'S PLACE WHILE HE'S ON HOLIDAY.
HOLIDAY!?
YEAH. HE STARTED A 'SIMPLE MOUSE' VLOG AND LIFESTYLE BRAND THAT MADE MILLIONS. HE'S GONE YACHTING WITH SUPER-RICH MOUSE.
WELL, COUNTRY MOUSE IS CERTAINLY MOVING UP IN THE WORLD! I'LL CALL HIM. PERHAPS I CAN JOIN THEM.
INCOMING CALL
TOWN MOUSE
NO ANSWER. HOW ODD. I'LL TRY HIM AGAIN LATER.

DYSTOPIAN ROAD SIGNS

PANIC

BEWARE: MUTATED WILDLIFE

LASER SECURITY ZONE

CAUTION: FERAL DRONE VEHICLES

FAILED UTOPIA

NO WEAPONIZED ANIMALS

WORSHIP THE AUTOMOBILE

ABANDON HOPE

WE'VE HAD OUR "INCITING INCIDENT" AND WE'RE ON THE "JOURNEY" SO IT SEEMS LIKE WE'LL BE HAVING A "CRISIS" ANY MINUTE NOW...
THIS QUEST WAS A LOT MORE FUN BEFORE YOU GOT THAT BOOK ON STORY STRUCTURE.

THE NINE ARCHETYPAL HEROINES
ROMANTIC
TRAGIC
MYSTERIOUS
HARD-BOILED
CYBORG
MURDEROUS LIBRARIAN
CAVEWOMAN
VICTORIAN TIME-TRAVELLER
INSECT QUEEN

JAWS
REBOOT POSSIBILITIES

BIGGER SHARK

IN SPACE

OPPOSITES

BUDDIES

EXISTENTIAL

OCCULT SYMBOLS OF THE ENGLISH COUNTRYSIDE

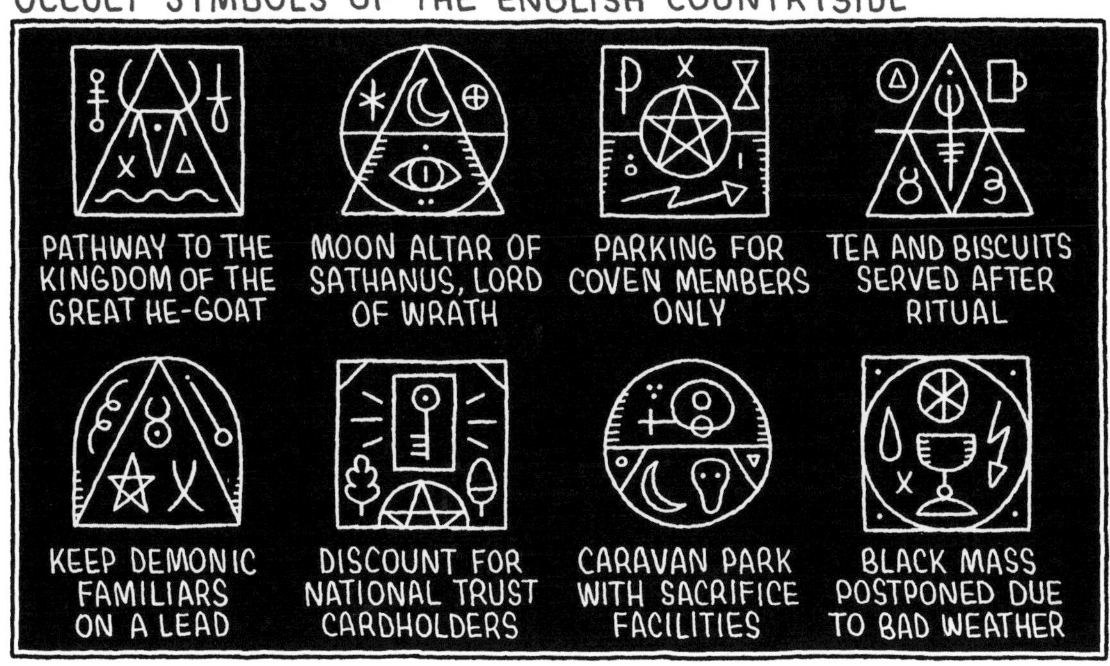

PATHWAY TO THE KINGDOM OF THE GREAT HE-GOAT
MOON ALTAR OF SATHANUS, LORD OF WRATH
PARKING FOR COVEN MEMBERS ONLY
TEA AND BISCUITS SERVED AFTER RITUAL
KEEP DEMONIC FAMILIARS ON A LEAD
DISCOUNT FOR NATIONAL TRUST CARDHOLDERS
CARAVAN PARK WITH SACRIFICE FACILITIES
BLACK MASS POSTPONED DUE TO BAD WEATHER

TIPS FOR GETTING YOUR NOVEL PUBLISHED DURING A SKELETON APOCALYPSE

TAKE THE INITIATIVE

PUBLISHERS RARELY READ UNSOLICITED MANUSCRIPTS BECAUSE THEY ARE TOO BUSY FIGHTING OFF MURDEROUS SKELETONS. SELF-PUBLISHING MIGHT BE YOUR BEST OPTION.

CREATE A BUZZ

WE ALL SPEND MOST OF OUR TIME IN CAVES AND CELLARS, HIDING FROM THE SKELETONS. WHY NOT TRY READING A CHAPTER OF YOUR BOOK TO THE CAPTIVE AUDIENCE?

CONSIDER YOUR AUDIENCE

THOUSANDS OF SKELETONS EMERGE THROUGH THE GATES OF HELL EVERY DAY. WITH HUMAN READERS IN DECLINE, IT MAY BE WORTH TAILORING YOUR WORK TO THE SKELETON MARKET.

THE SNOOTY BOOKSHOP
YES, WE DO HAVE A COPY OF THE BOOK YOU'RE LOOKING FOR. YOU'LL FIND IT IN THE "VASTLY OVERRATED" SECTION OF THE "SO-CALLED CLASSICS" DEPARTMENT.

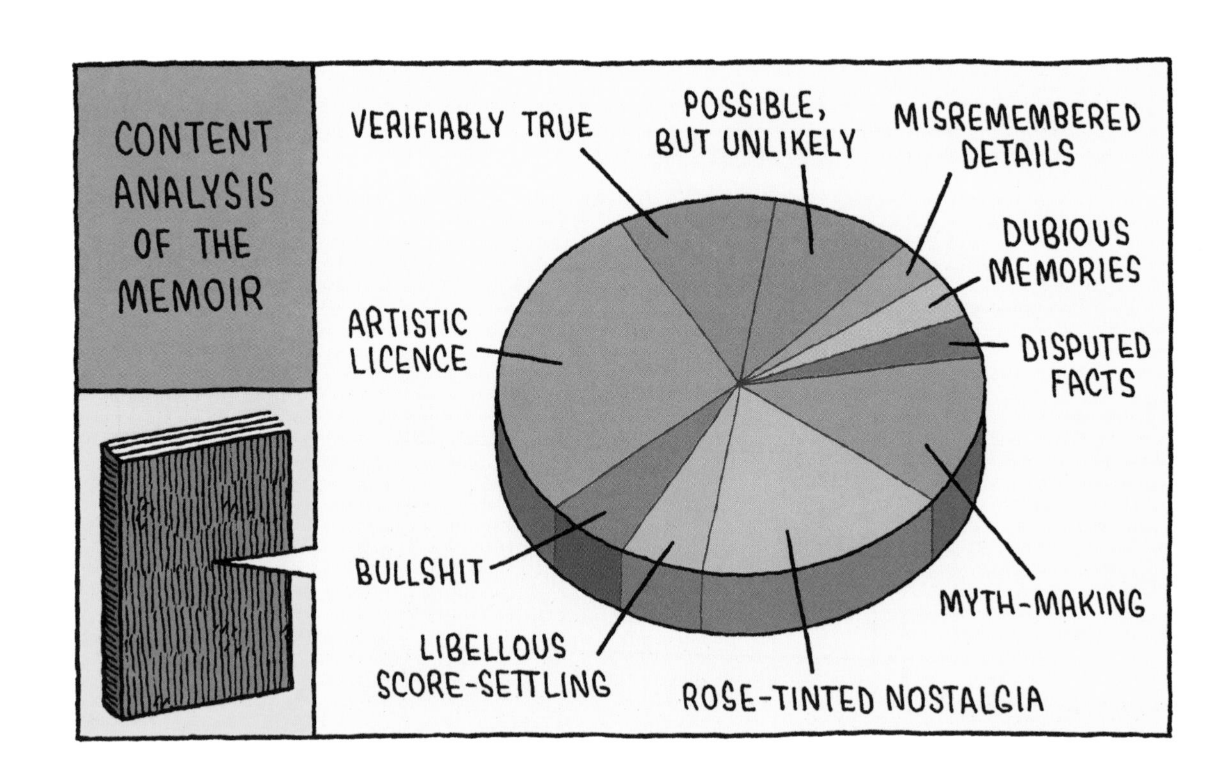
CONTENT ANALYSIS OF THE MEMOIR
VERIFIABLY TRUE
POSSIBLE, BUT UNLIKELY
MISREMEMBERED DETAILS
DUBIOUS MEMORIES
DISPUTED FACTS
MYTH-MAKING
ROSE-TINTED NOSTALGIA
LIBELLOUS SCORE-SETTLING
BULLSHIT
ARTISTIC LICENCE

HI, JUST THOUGHT I'D DROP BY AND SEE HOW THE MANUSCRIPT'S COMING ALONG...
FINE THANKS, GOD.
YOU'RE PUTTING IN LOTS OF-
FIDDLY BITS. LOTS OF FIDDLY BITS. I KNOW HOW MUCH YOU LIKE THEM.
AND FANCY BIG-
YES, YES. FANCY BIG LETTERS WITH PICTURES INSIDE THEM. JUST LIKE YOU ASKED FOR.
I'M QUITE BUSY, ACTUALLY.
OF COURSE. SORRY. I'LL LEAVE YOU TO GET ON WITH IT.
THANK YOU.

RECENTLY DISCOVERED CLASSICAL GREEK VASES
SOCRATES WITH TIME MACHINE AND DINOSAUR EGG.
PLATO DEMONSTRATING THE YO-YO, HULA-HOOP AND SKATEBOARD.
ARISTOTLE AND ROBO-ARISTOTLE.

A
B
DO YOU HAVE A NAME?
NOPE. YOU?
NO, BUT I THINK THIS MUST BE A FIRST DRAFT. I EXPECT THE AUTHOR WILL GIVE US NAMES LATER.
OH GOOD.
UNLESS...
UNLESS WHAT?
UNLESS THIS IS ONE OF THOSE EXPERIMENTAL STORIES WHERE NOBODY HAS A NAME AND NOTHING EVER HAPPENS.
A
B
OH DEAR.
A
B

POETRY BY LEFT-HANDED SCANDINAVIANS
COOKBOOKS BY DOG-OWNING ATHEISTS
THRILLERS BY BEARDED WRITERS UNDER 5'6"
SHORT STORIES BY DIVORCED CELEBRITIES
EROTICA BY AUTHORS WITH A NUT ALLERGY

WILLIAM MORRIS AND HIS REVOLUTIONARY BEARD
BEARD, HERE COMES LORD WORPLESDON. CAN YOU PLEASE TRY TO KEEP YOUR REVOLUTIONARY VIEWS TO YOURSELF?
NEVER!
AH, MORRIS. HOW'S MY WALLPAPER COMING ALONG?
VERY WELL, YOUR LORDSHIP.
POMPOUS CAPITALIST LEECH!
WHAT!?
I SAID: I'LL HAVE TWENTY ROLLS READY BY THURSDAY.
GOOD.
NOW I MUST GET BACK TO WORK ON LADY MALVERN'S FABRIC SAMPLES.
COWARDLY BOURGEOIS LICKSPITTLE!

2513 AD
AH! HOW GOOD IT FEELS TO PASS ALONG THIS ANCIENT PATHWAY...
2113 AD
TO FOLLOW IN THE FOOTSTEPS OF THE SIMPLE FOLK OF THE PAST...
2013 AD
WHY, I CAN ALMOST HEAR THE VOICES OF MY ANCESTORS ECHOING DOWN THE YEARS.
13 BC
UGH. MORE BLOODY RAIN.

HOW TO SUBMIT YOUR SPY NOVEL FOR PUBLICATION

TRANSFER THE NOVEL TO MICROFILM AND DESTROY ALL OTHER COPIES. TRAVEL TO VIENNA BY TRAIN.

HIDE THE MICROFILM IN THE POCKET OF A RAINCOAT AND LEAVE IT IN THE CLOAKROOM OF THE OPERA HOUSE.

PLACE A MESSAGE IN THE TIMES WHICH MENTIONS DAFFODILS, THEN RENT A ROOM UNDER THE NAME 'BROWNING'.

A CLANDESTINE MEETING WITH AN EDITOR WILL BE ARRANGED BY AN INTERMEDIARY FROM THE SWISS EMBASSY.

AN X-RAY OF MY SUITCASE

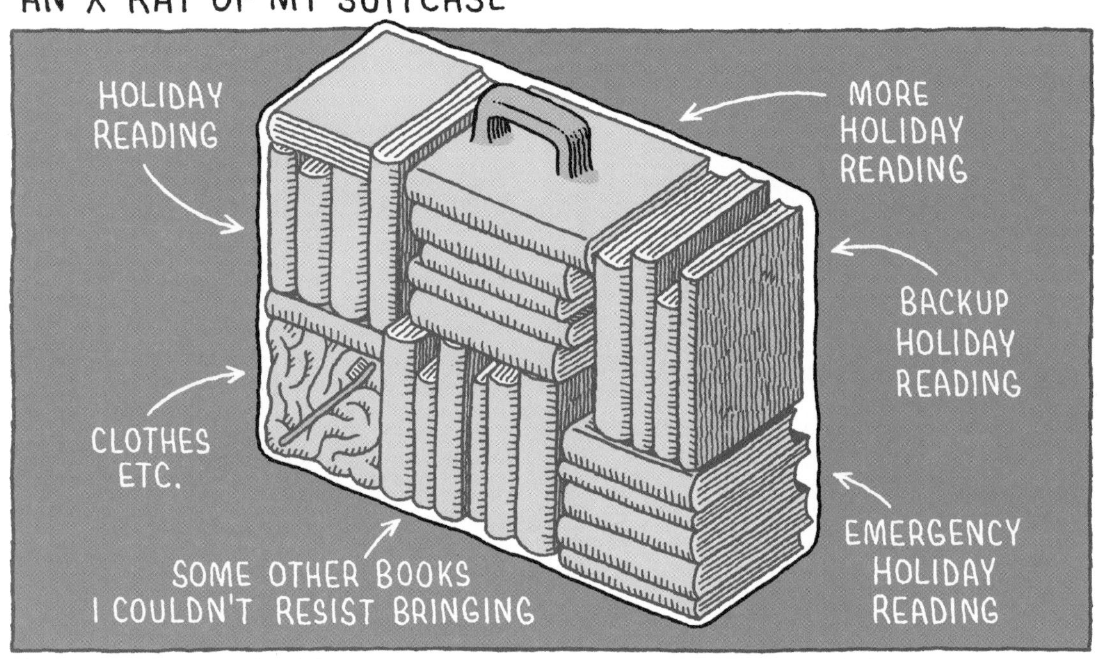

THE AUTEUR DIRECTS A SUPERHERO MOVIE

READING POSTURE

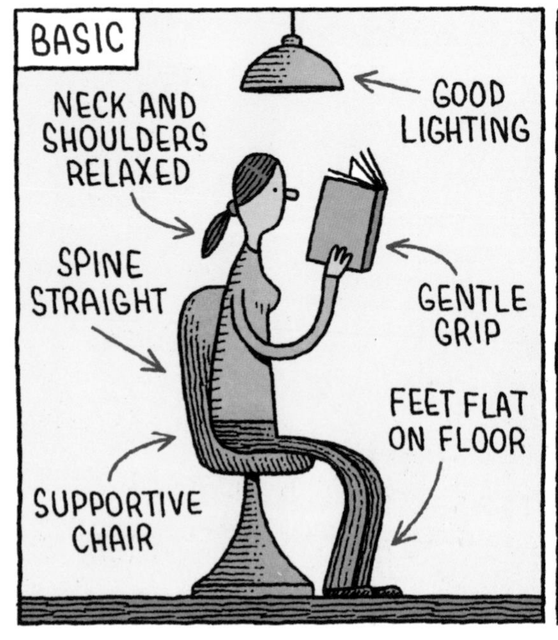
BASIC
GOOD LIGHTING
NECK AND SHOULDERS RELAXED
SPINE STRAIGHT
GENTLE GRIP
FEET FLAT ON FLOOR
SUPPORTIVE CHAIR

ADVANCED
X-RAY VISION
YOGIC READING TRANCE
TELEKINETIC BOOK CONTROL
FORCEFIELD
EXTRASENSORY PERCEPTION
LEVITATING

PROMOTIONAL STICKERS FOR NOVELS

THE VOICE OF A GENERATION

UNPUT-DOWNABLE!

BY THE AUTHOR OF A MUCH BETTER, MORE FAMOUS NOVEL

POSSIBLY WORTH BUYING IF IT'S IN ONE OF THOSE 3 FOR THE PRICE OF 2 OFFERS

A BIT LIKE THAT OTHER BOOK YOU LIKED

YOU WON'T ENJOY IT, BUT PEOPLE WILL THINK YOU'RE CLEVER

OCCASIONALLY-PUTDOWNABLE

HONESTLY, NOT AS BAD AS EVERYONE SAYS IT IS

CURRENTLY ON SHOW IN OUR MUSEUM
TEN OBJECTS THAT CHANGED THE WORLD
NINE IMPORTANT CULTURAL ARTEFACTS
THIRTEEN LESS IMPORTANT CULTURAL ARTEFACTS
ELEVEN FRANKLY MEDIOCRE ITEMS
TWENTY OTHER BITS & BOBS WE HAD LYING AROUND
FOURTEEN THINGS WE SHOULD PROBABLY GET RID OF

EARLY APPEARANCES OF THE SMARTPHONE IN LITERATURE

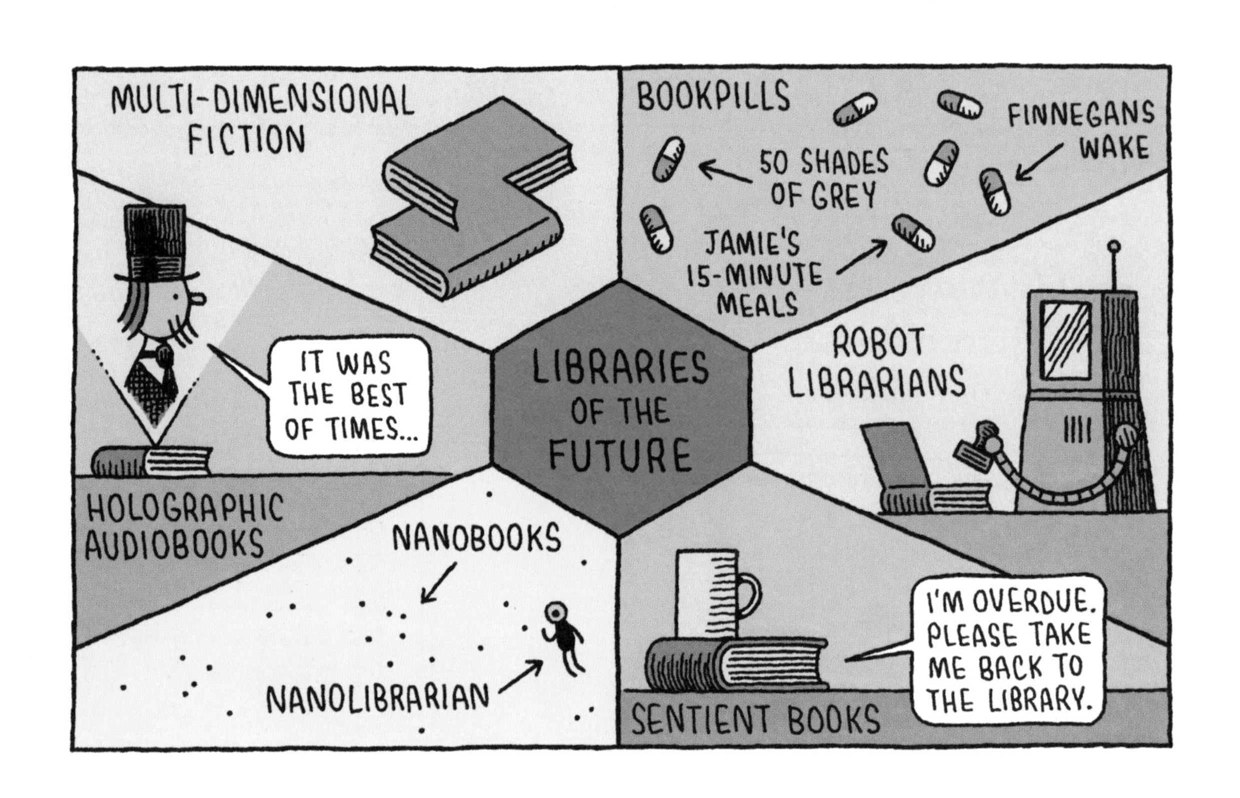
MULTI-DIMENSIONAL FICTION
BOOKPILLS
50 SHADES OF GREY
FINNEGANS WAKE
JAMIE'S 15-MINUTE MEALS
IT WAS THE BEST OF TIMES...
LIBRARIES OF THE FUTURE
ROBOT LIBRARIANS
HOLOGRAPHIC AUDIOBOOKS
NANOBOOKS
NANOLIBRARIAN
I'M OVERDUE. PLEASE TAKE ME BACK TO THE LIBRARY.
SENTIENT BOOKS

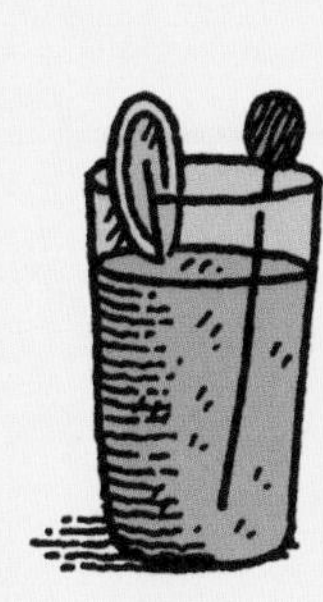

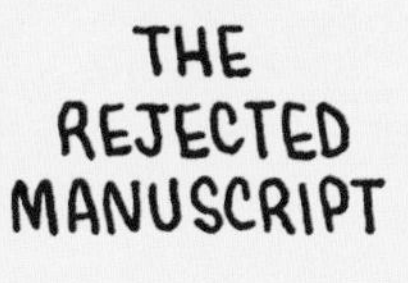
HARD DAY AT THE WRITING DESK?
UNWIND WITH ONE OF OUR AUTHORS' COCKTAILS
THE REJECTED MANUSCRIPT
THE MEDDLING PUBLISHER
THE DREADFUL REVIEW
THE DISAPPOINTING SALES FIGURES

SOME UNFORTUNATE ERRORS IN THE NEW JAMES BOND NOVEL

BOND'S SIGNATURE DRINK IS A VODKA MARTINI, NOT "A LARGE RASPBERRY SLUSH PUPPIE."

BOND'S WEAPON OF CHOICE IS THE WALTHER PPK, NOT "THE NERF SUPER SOAKER MAX."

BOND'S PREFERRED GAME IS BACCARAT CHEMIN DE FER, NOT "ADVANCED DUNGEONS AND DRAGONS."

COST BREAKDOWN OF A SLIM VOLUME OF POETRY
RETAILER'S CUT
PRINTING
SALES DEPT.
BRIBES
SLUSH FUND
DISTRIBUTION
EXCESSIVE BONUSES
CHAMPAGNE
FOCUS GROUPS
COMPANY JET
CORPORATE ESPIONAGE
POET'S ROYALTY
POET'S ROYALTY BREAKDOWN
AGENT
MANAGER
STYLIST
MANAGER'S AGENT
AGENT'S MANAGER
CHAMPAGNE
HANDMADE NOTEBOOKS
ANTIQUE QUILL PENS
MASSEUR
SUSHI CHEF
FLOWERS
ARTISANAL INK
ICE SCULPTURES

SOME HORRIFYINGLY FIENDISH CROSSWORDS

THE MIND-BREAKER
Nº. 27,504

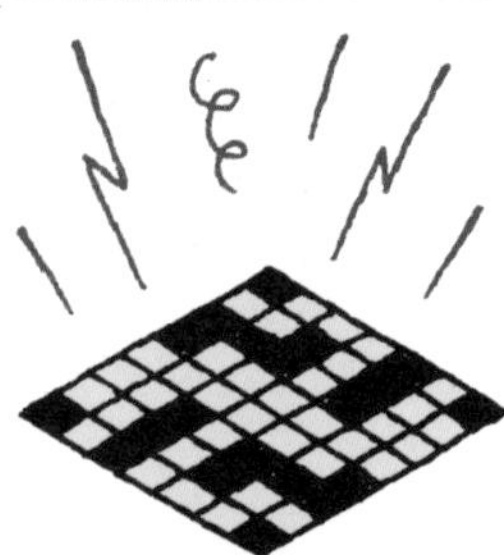

SO INFURIATING THAT NO-ONE EVER SOLVED IT WITHOUT GOING MAD.

THE HAUNTED PUZZLE
Nº. 29,088

CONTAINS A GHOST WHO HAUNTS THE SOLVER UNTIL THE PUZZLE IS COMPLETE.

THE GATEWAY
Nº. 30,104

COMPLETION OPENS A PORTAL TO HELL.

THE BLACK CROSSWORD
Nº. 31,322

NO CLUES.
NO WHITE SQUARES.
LIFE IS POINTLESS.

JONATHAN FRANZEN SAYS NO

JONATHAN! OUR MARKETING AND NEW MEDIA TEAMS HAVE COME UP WITH SOME REALLY INNOVATIVE CROSS-PLATFORM STRATEGIES TO PROMOTE YOUR NEW BOOK! SHALL I TELL YOU ABOUT THEM?

NO

NEW ON YOUR E-READER: USED BOOK SIMULATION

ODOURS
NICOTINE.
OLD BOOK SMELL.
BRANDY AND CIGARS IN A LEATHER ARMCHAIR.
PREVIOUS READERS' BOOKMARKS
TICKET STUB.
MELANCHOLY REMINDER OF TIME'S CONSTANT MARCH.
PORNOGRAPHIC PHOTOGRAPH.
SIMULATED DAMAGE
COFFEE STAINS.
MISSING PAGES.
CATASTROPHIC SPINE COLLAPSE.
MARGINALIA
OCCASIONAL UNDERLINING.
ENTIRE PH.D. IN MARGINS.
CHILDISH SCRIBBLES.
MYSTERIOUS CODE.

THE RE-HANG IN THE MUSEUM'S M.C. ESCHER GALLERY IS NOT GOING WELL

THE POETRY GENE: A TIMELINE

2014

THE POETRY GENE IS IDENTIFIED.

2016

IT IS SUCCESSFULLY TRANSPLANTED INTO A FRUIT FLY.

TODAY I FLY.

TOMORROW I WILL DIE.

2017

A GENETICALLY MODIFIED MOUSE WRITES A HAIKU.

WINTER MOONLIGHT-

A BRIE WAITS SILENTLY

UPON THE SIDEBOARD.

2020

AN ORANGUTAN WINS THE T.S. ELIOT PRIZE FOR POETRY.

THE WRITER
HAHA. THIS IS FUNNY.
MAYBE NOT HILARIOUS, BUT FUNNY.
IT IS SORT OF FUNNY.
IT SEEMED FUNNY WHEN I THOUGHT OF IT.
MAYBE IT'S NOT FUNNY.
NO. IT IS FUNNY.
I'M REALLY VERY SURE IT'S FUNNY.
DEFINITELY
THE READER
HAHA.

PROCRASTINATION FOR CREATIVE WRITERS, A 10-WEEK COURSE

TOPICS COVERED INCLUDE:

- WORKSPACE ARRANGEMENT
- PRE-WRITING RITUALS
- STATIONERY CHOICES
- WAITING FOR INSPIRATION
- SNACKS AND BEVERAGES
- FINDING THE PERFECT FONT
- WORKSPACE REARRANGEMENT
- UTILIZING SOCIAL MEDIA
- PAUSES, TEA BREAKS AND NAPS
- ADVANCED WORKSPACE REARRANGEMENT

THE AUTHOR AND THE TRANSLATOR

TRANSLATION:

"I WOULD LIKE TO CONGRATULATE YOU ON YOUR BRILLIANT TRANSLATION OF MY NOVEL."

TRANSLATION:

"THE CREATIVE LIBERTIES WHICH YOU HAVE TAKEN WITH MY TEXT HAVE GREATLY IMPROVED IT."

TRANSLATION:

"IT IS MY HOPE THAT WE WILL HAVE THE OPPORTUNITY TO WORK TOGETHER AGAIN SOON."

SHAKESPEARE ADAPTATION GENERATOR

CHOOSE ONE ITEM FROM EACH COLUMN TO CREATE AN INNOVATIVE PRODUCTION IDEA!

SILENT	KUNG FU	HAMLET	WITH A NEW ENDING
NUDE	BICYCLING	MACBETH	ON MARS
FRENCH	ROBOT	RICHARD III	ABOARD A SPEEDBOAT
COCKNEY	ZOMBIE	OTHELLO	ON WALL STREET
STALINIST	HIP HOP	KING LEAR	WITH DINOSAURS
DRUNK	COWBOY	ROMEO & JULIET	IN A CAR PARK

INNOVATIONS FOR THE MODERN NOVELIST
RESEARCH-DRONE
DICTATION-BOT
PUBLICITY-COPTER
ROBO-ASSISTANT
IDEA-DROID
ELECTRO-PLOTTER
MECHA-AGENT
CYBER-EDITOR

MISTER NATURE WRITER

MISTER NATURE WRITER IS IN A BAD MOOD. I'M SURE ONE OF HIS NICE WALKS IN THE COUNTRYSIDE WILL CHEER HIM UP.

MISTER NATURE WRITER IS BURNING HIS CLOTHES SO THAT HE CAN LIVE LIKE AN ANIMAL IN THE WOODS. I HOPE HE DOESN'T CATCH A COLD.

DO BE CAREFUL WITH YOUR BOW AND POISON-TIPPED ARROWS, MISTER NATURE WRITER, I HEAR OTHER PEOPLE IN THE WOOD.

THE OTHER PEOPLE MUST HAVE GONE HOME, AND MISTER NATURE WRITER HAS MADE HIMSELF A DELICIOUS STEW. GOODNIGHT MISTER NATURE WRITER!

THE HUMOUR ARCHAEOLOGISTS

AN E-READER ARRIVES ON THE KITCHEN SHELF...

PLANNING NEIL GAIMAN'S 'NORSE MYTHOLOGY' BOOK TOUR
AH, HERE COMES ODIN. HE'LL BE LOOKING AFTER YOU ON THE TOUR.
WHERE'S SOPHIE?
MATERNITY LEAVE.
I AM ODIN OF ASGARD! I SWEAR UPON GUNGNIR, MY MIGHTY SPEAR, TO PROTECT THEE WITH MY LIFE!
UH, THANKS... IT'S MORE A CASE OF BOOKING TAXIS AND FINDING SOMEWHERE NICE FOR DINNER.
WE SHALL RIDE UPON SLEIPNIR, MY EIGHT-LEGGED HORSE, DINE ON MEAT CAUGHT BY MY WOLVES AND DRINK FROM THE SKULLS OF YOUR ENEMIES!
I'M NOT SURE THAT I HAVE ENEMIES... MAYBE SOME INTERNET TROLLS.
TROLLS!! I SHALL NOT REST UNTIL WE ARE KNEE-DEEP IN THEIR CORPSES!
WELL, PERHAPS WE COULD SLAY A FEW TROLLS BETWEEN BOOKSHOPS...

ROGUE BIBLIOPHILE 2500 AD
LEVEL ONE
OBJECTIVE: SURVIVE THE WILDERNESS
LEVEL TWO
OBJECTIVE: BREACH THE CITY WALLS
LEVEL THREE
OBJECTIVE: LOCATE THE LIBRARY
LEVELS FOUR TO 84,000,000
OBJECTIVE: READ THE BOOKS
CONTROLS
A LASER
B JETPACK
X TURN PAGE
Y NEW BOOK

AN EXCLUSIVE EXCERPT FROM 'THE WOLF HALL FUN BOOK' BY HILARY MANTEL
SPOT THE DIFFERENCE
CAN YOU SPOT THE THREE DIFFERENCES BETWEEN THOMAS CROMWELL AND HIS PORTRAIT?
MAZE
LEAD KING HENRY TO HIS TRYST WITH ANNE BOLEYN AVOIDING THE QUEEN AND THE FRENCH AMBASSADOR.
ART
DESIGN A NICE NEW HAT FOR CARDINAL WOLSEY.

OUR PRODUCTION OF THE TEMPEST IS PRESENTED AT FOUR DIFFICULTY LEVELS
EASY
FAMOUS HOLLYWOOD ACTORS
EXPENSIVE SPECIAL-EFFECTS
SHORT VERSION OF THE TEXT
MODERATE
COMPLETE, UNEDITED TEXT
CLASSICAL ACTORS
ELIZABETHAN MUSIC
CANDLELIGHT
CHALLENGING
REWORKED PLOT
AUDIENCE PARTICIPATION
MIME
PUPPETS
NUDITY
HIP-HOP
EXTREME
MINIMAL SET
SOUNDTRACK OF ABSTRACT NOISE
SCRIPT REWRITTEN BY AN ALGORITHM
EIGHTEEN HOURS LONG

WHY SO GLUM?
I'VE BEEN ADAPTED.

OH, COME ALONG. BAD ADAPTATIONS HAPPEN TO THE BEST OF US. IN THE EIGHTIES I WAS MADE INTO A GERMAN TV MOVIE STARRING DAVID HASSELHOFF.
IT'S MUCH WORSE THAN THAT. LOOK AT THE REVIEWS.

A MASTERPIECE!
THAT RARE THING: A FILM WHICH WHOLLY SURPASSES ITS SOURCE MATERIAL.
OH DEAR.

POETRY ANTHOLOGIES FOR PEOPLE WHO DON'T LIKE POEMS
LOOKS NICE ON A SHELF!
A PRETTY BOOK OF POETRY
MAINLY PICTURES!
A SHORT BOOK OF POETRY
VERY FEW POEMS!
GIVE IT AWAY!
A GIFT BOOK OF POETRY
NO NEED TO READ!

ELDERLY
PEOPLE

ANGRY ELDERLY
PEOPLE

ELDERLY
MOB

ELDERLY
REVOLUTIONARIES

ELDERLY
ARMY

OUR ELDERLY
OVERLORDS

THE ART OF THE MENU
BEGINNING
THOUGHT
ANGST
DESPAIR
FURY
EXHAUSTION
INSPIRATION
STRUGGLE
TRIUMPH!
CHICKEN
and CHIPS
or
STEAK PIE

COUNTRYSIDE TERROR!

THIS SEASON'S HOT PUBLISHING TREND: SPINSTERS!

An interview with a Cultural Teddy Bear

MY FORTHCOMING COUNTER-FACTUAL HISTORY BOOKS

PLANNED EXTENSION OF THE ART GALLERY

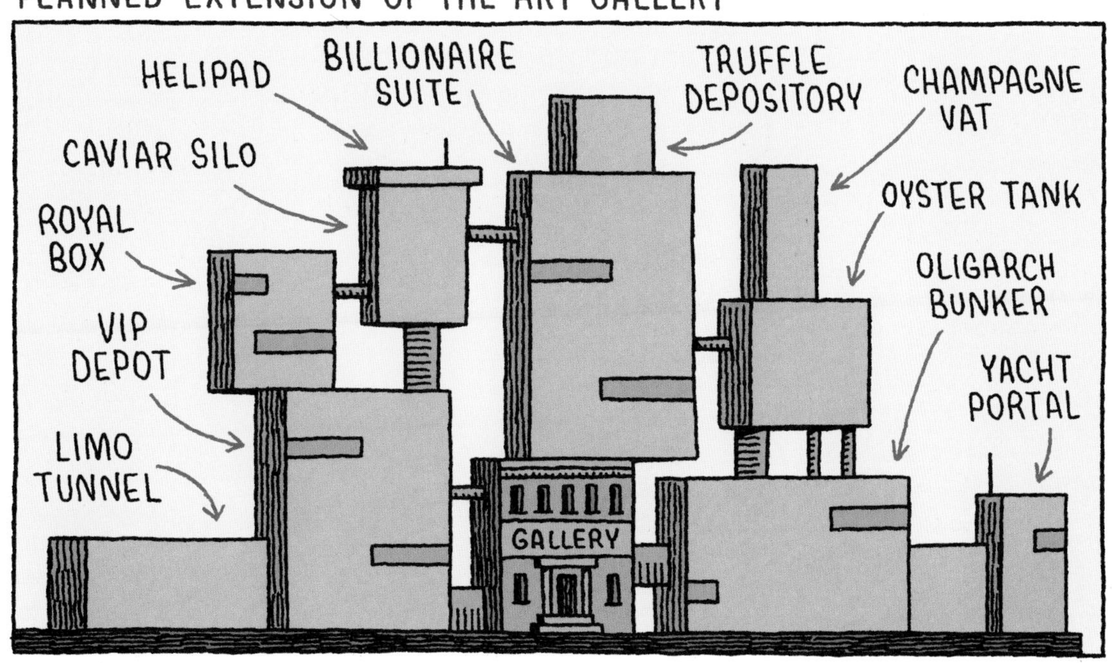

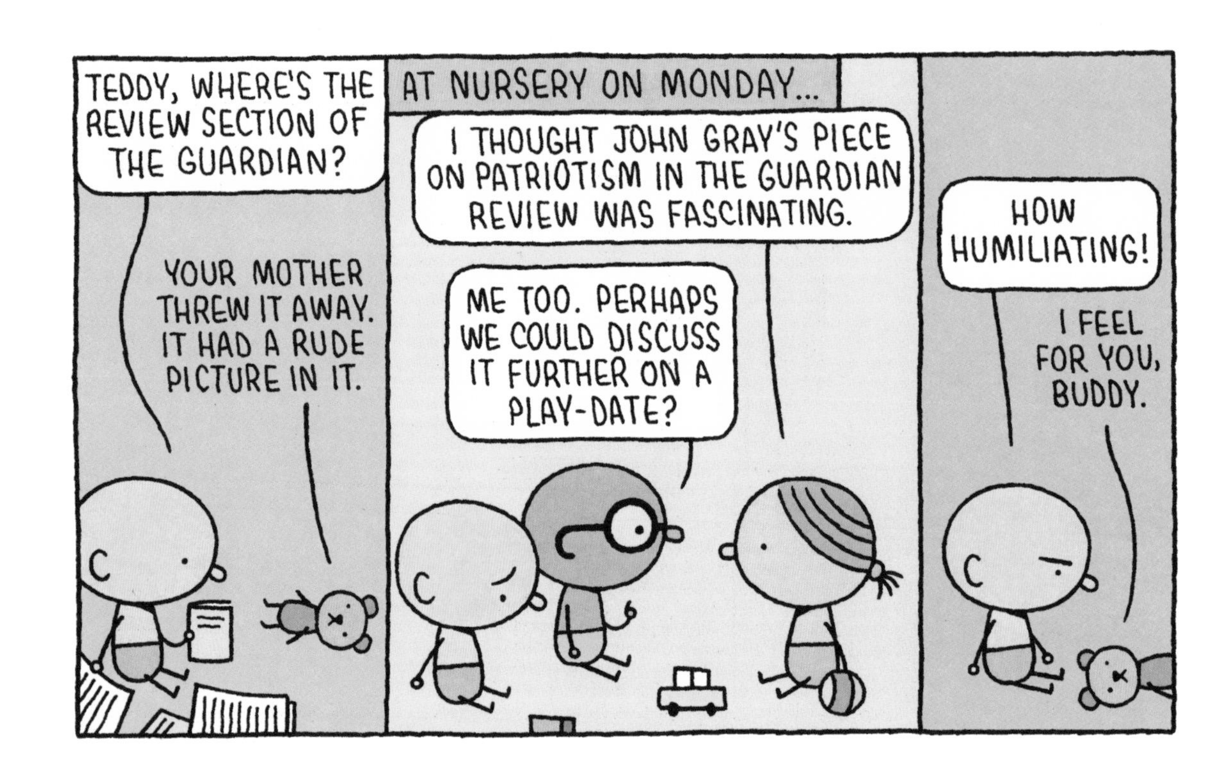
TEDDY, WHERE'S THE REVIEW SECTION OF THE GUARDIAN?
YOUR MOTHER THREW IT AWAY. IT HAD A RUDE PICTURE IN IT.
AT NURSERY ON MONDAY...
I THOUGHT JOHN GRAY'S PIECE ON PATRIOTISM IN THE GUARDIAN REVIEW WAS FASCINATING.
ME TOO. PERHAPS WE COULD DISCUSS IT FURTHER ON A PLAY-DATE?
HOW HUMILIATING!
I FEEL FOR YOU, BUDDY.

LAST-MINUTE CHANGES TO THE POLITICIAN'S SPEECH

ERRORS COMMONLY MADE BY INEXPERIENCED MURDER-MYSTERY NOVELISTS
NOT ENOUGH SUSPECTS
NOBODY GETS MURDERED
TOO MANY BUTLERS
DETECTIVE JUST GIVES UP

SUBSCRIBE TODAY!

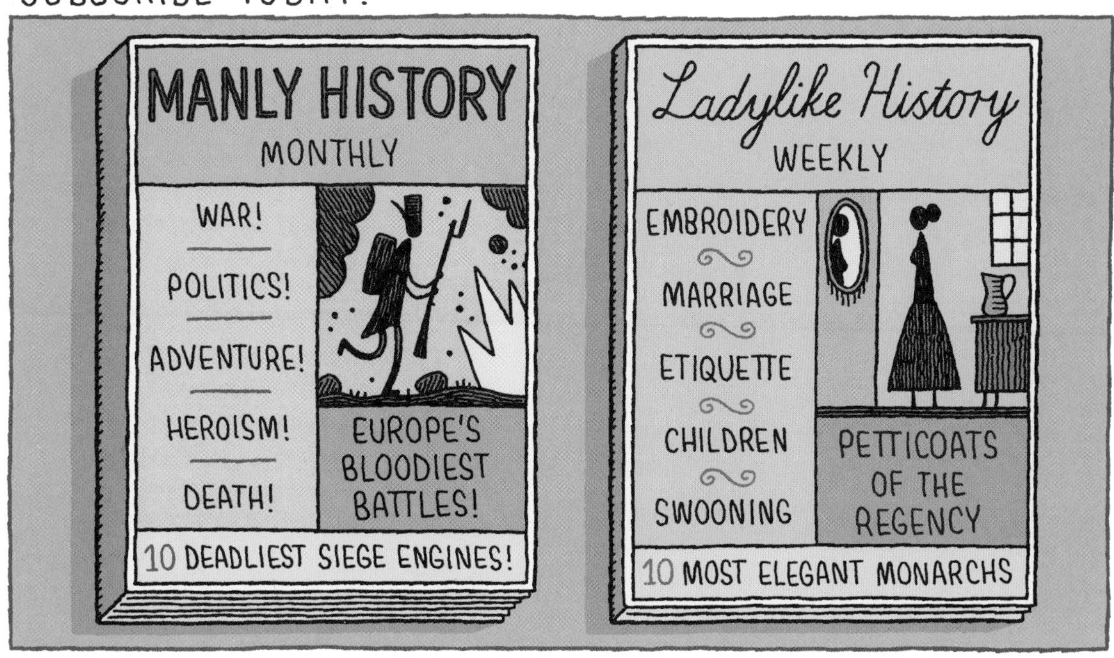

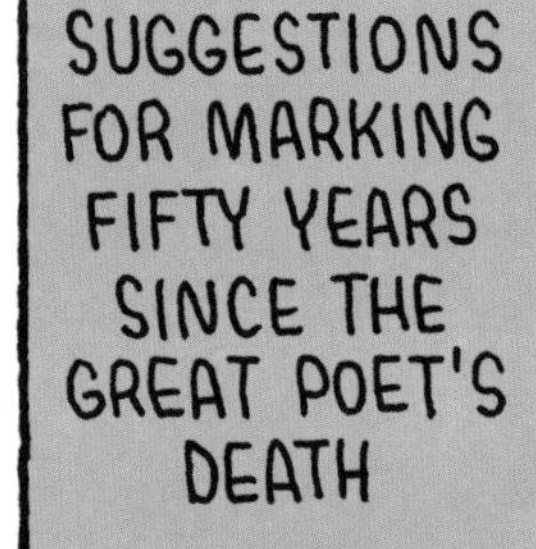
SUGGESTIONS FOR MARKING FIFTY YEARS SINCE THE GREAT POET'S DEATH

PLAQUE ON CHILDHOOD HOME

I
II
III
ANNOTATED EDITION OF THE COMPLETE POEMS

BALLOON PARADE

SCURRILOUS NEW BIOGRAPHY

HAPPY MEAL TOY

INTERACTIVE HOLOGRAM

POEMS USED IN A SERIES OF CAR ADVERTISEMENTS

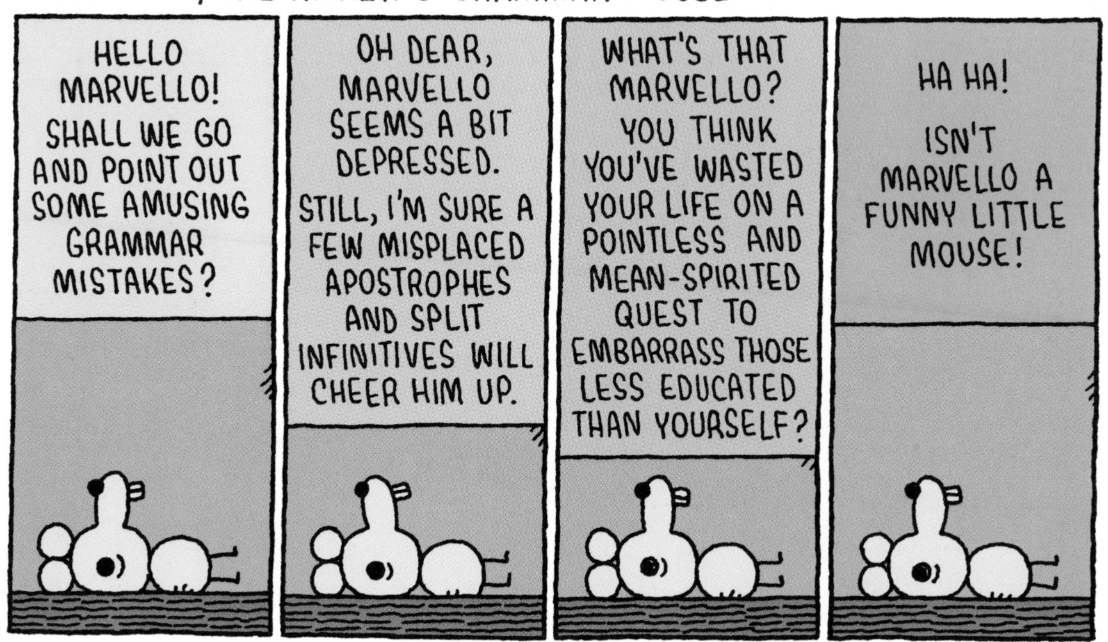
MARVELLO, THE AMAZING GRAMMAR MOUSE
HELLO MARVELLO! SHALL WE GO AND POINT OUT SOME AMUSING GRAMMAR MISTAKES?
OH DEAR, MARVELLO SEEMS A BIT DEPRESSED. STILL, I'M SURE A FEW MISPLACED APOSTROPHES AND SPLIT INFINITIVES WILL CHEER HIM UP.
WHAT'S THAT MARVELLO? YOU THINK YOU'VE WASTED YOUR LIFE ON A POINTLESS AND MEAN-SPIRITED QUEST TO EMBARRASS THOSE LESS EDUCATED THAN YOURSELF?
HA HA! ISN'T MARVELLO A FUNNY LITTLE MOUSE!

I'M BEGINNING TO SUSPECT THAT OUR AUTHOR IS TRYING TO TURN 'ITALIAN COOKERY FOR BEGINNERS' INTO THAT DARK, GRITTY THRILLER SHE'S ALWAYS WANTED TO WRITE.

CAN YOU LEAD THE AUTOBIOGRAPHICAL NOVELIST TO THE LITERARY PRIZE, AVOIDING HIS ANGRY FRIENDS AND RELATIVES?

HAVE YOU HEARD? WE'RE GETTING A WOOD-BURNING STOVE!!
OH, RIGHT.
DON'T YOU SEE WHAT THIS MEANS? WE'RE GOING UP IN THE WORLD! COUSCOUS! ESPRESSO! FARROW AND BALL! BBC 4! I ALWAYS KNEW I WAS DESTINED FOR BETTER THINGS!
A FEW WEEKS LATER...
WHERE'S LAMP?
DUNNO.
TAKE ME

I WISH THAT
THE AUTHOR WOULD
JUST PICK A GENRE
AND STICK TO IT.

WAR AND PEACE CLICKBAIT

This man inherited his father's fortune. You won't **believe** what happened next!

29 incredible facts about Napoleon Bonaparte. N°4 will **shock** you!

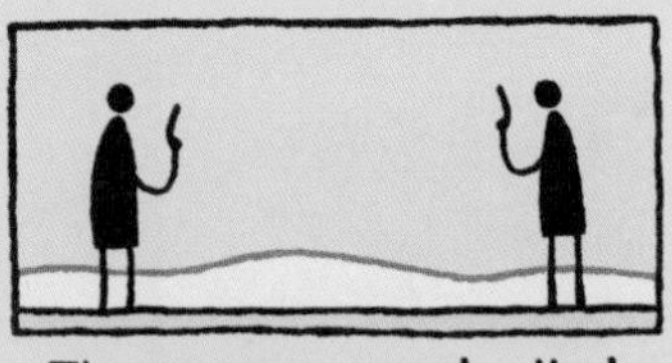

These two men **duelled**. The outcome will surprise you!

Ten signs that you are becoming a **freemason**!

These russian aristocrats got engaged. What happened next will **blow your mind**!

This saintly peasant's simple wisdom will make you question **everything**!

THE EASILY INFLUENCED NOVELIST'S CHARACTERS
HE'S BEEN READING KAFKA AGAIN, HASN'T HE?
'FRAID SO.

MR. MARXIST AND MR. CAPITALIST
MR. MARXIST! YOU HAVE TO HELP! THE PEOPLE HAVE RISEN UP AGAINST ME!
REALLY!?
I'VE BEEN SUCH AN IDIOT! YOU WERE RIGHT ALL ALONG.
THIS IS INCREDIBLE!
HA HA!
FOOLED YOU!
EVERYBODY STILL LOVES CAPITALISM!
HA
HA

DAVID BOWIE'S FORGOTTEN NON-FICTION BOOKS
MAJOR TOM'S
101 things to do on a long journey
The Red Pepper and Milk Diet
by the Thin White Duke
My first ZIGGY STARDUST word book
Ziggy
spider
mars
Dress for Success with Aladdin Sane
The TIN MACHINE cookbook

THE LIFE OF A MEMOIRIST

WHAT ARE YOU DOING HERE?
I THOUGHT THIS WAS A CARTOON ABOUT FOOTBALL.

FOOTBALL? YOU'VE GOT TO BE JOKING!
IT'S ALL ABOUT BOOKS ROUND HERE, MATE.
SHOVE OFF BACK TO THE SPORTS SECTION!

SOB!

LET'S DESIGN A BOOK COVER!
YOU WILL NEED:
PENCIL
RUBBER
DICE
STEP 1: DRAW YOUR COVER
NOW GO TO STEP 2...
STEP 2: ROLL THE DICE TO GET FEEDBACK
1. THE MARKETING TEAM DON'T LIKE IT, GO BACK TO STEP 1 AND START AGAIN.
2. THE ART DIRECTOR THINKS IT'S TOO MINIMAL, GO BACK AND ADD SOMETHING.
3. THE AUTHOR LIKES [ROLL AGAIN: 1. DOGS 2. CARS 3. NUDES 4. SHOES 5. GUNS 6. FISH], GO BACK AND ADD ONE.
4. THE FOCUS GROUP SAY IT'S CONFUSING, GO BACK AND SIMPLIFY IT.
5. THE PUBLISHER WANTS MORE IMPACT, GO BACK AND MAKE THE TEXT BIGGER.
6. EVERYONE LOVES IT! YOU WIN!

SPORTSPLAGUE!
A MYSTERY VIRUS IS TURNING EVERY-ONE INTO SPORTS-OBSESSED ZOMBIES. NICK AND MARC ARE SAFELY HIDDEN IN A BUNKER...
OH NO! I FORGOT MY COPY OF ULYSSES!
BOOKS
DON'T GO OUT, NICK! IT'S TOO DANGEROUS!
WHAT'S THE POINT OF LIVING WITH-OUT GREAT ART?
LATER...
MARC! I'M BACK! THE ZOMBIES WERE TOO EXCITED ABOUT THE MATCH TO NOTICE ME!
MARC?
YOU'RE JUST IN TIME, NICK. KICK-OFF IS IN FIVE MINUTES.
NOOOOO!

IF CHARLES DICKENS WERE ALIVE TODAY

"DAMMIT! THIS CASE IS GOING NOWHERE." THOUGHT THE DETECTIVE, AS HE STUDIED THE EVIDENCE PINNED TO THE WALL AND
~~LIT HIS FIRST CIGARETTE OF THE DAY~~
~~POURED HIS FIRST COFFEE OF THE DAY~~
BLENDED HIS FIRST AVOCADO AND KALE SMOOTHIE OF THE DAY.

The Nature Critic shares his expert knowledge

ENJOY A MORE AUTHENTIC SHAKESPEAREAN EXPERIENCE!
PICK AN INSTRUCTION CARD AS YOU ENTER THE THEATRE

YOU GOT DRUNK
AT THE TAVERN

THROW FRUIT AT
THE STAGE AND
INSULT THE ACTORS

YOU ARE SET UPON
BY CUTPURSES

GIVE AWAY ALL
YOUR MONEY AND
VALUABLES

YOU ARE SUSPECTED
OF BEING A CATHOLIC

FIND SOMEWHERE
TO HIDE FOR THE
ENTIRE EVENING

YOU'VE SPENT ALL
YOUR MONEY AT
THE BROTHEL

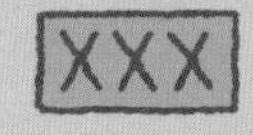

GO HOME
IMMEDIATELY

YOU HAVE THE POX

WRITHE IN TERRIBLE
PAIN THROUGHOUT
THE PERFORMANCE

AN ARISTOCRAT TAKES
A DISLIKE TO YOU

APOLOGISE TO
EVERYONE AND LEAVE
AT THE INTERVAL

ALL CHARACTERS WAIT HERE
RESEARCH IN PROGRESS

J.G. BALLARD'S BOOKS FOR CHILDREN WERE NOT A SUCCESS
Ballard the Bear
has a numb, medicated existence in a hellish techno-utopia.
Ballard the Bear
finds barbarism and perversion beneath the thin veneer of civilisation.
Ballard the Bear
fights for survival in the mutated ecosystem of a post-disaster world.

BEFORE BECOMING AN AUTHOR, CONSIDER THE HEALTH HAZARDS
SORE HAND FROM SIGNING LATEST BESTSELLER.
BAD BACK FROM CARRYING ROYALTIES TO THE BANK.
HEAD INJURY FROM COLLAPSING AWARDS SHELF.
PAPERCUT FROM YET ANOTHER RAVE REVIEW.
EXHAUSTED BY CONSTANT STREAM OF AMAZING IDEAS.

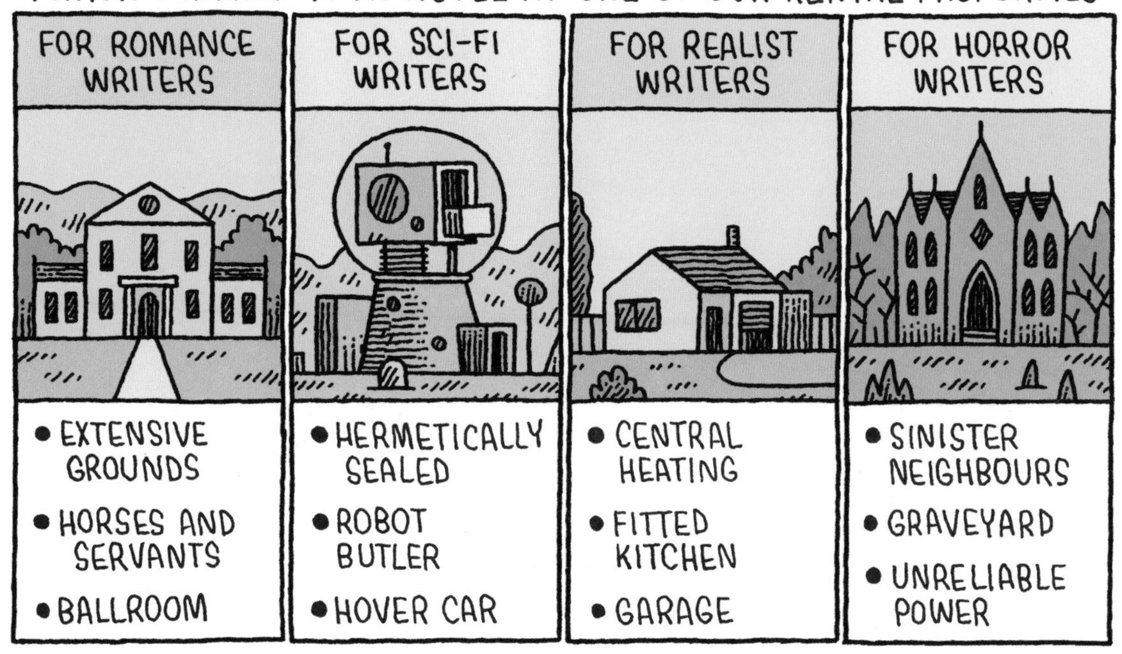
FINISH WRITING YOUR NOVEL AT ONE OF OUR RENTAL PROPERTIES
FOR ROMANCE WRITERS
• EXTENSIVE GROUNDS
• HORSES AND SERVANTS
• BALLROOM
FOR SCI-FI WRITERS
• HERMETICALLY SEALED
• ROBOT BUTLER
• HOVER CAR
FOR REALIST WRITERS
• CENTRAL HEATING
• FITTED KITCHEN
• GARAGE
FOR HORROR WRITERS
• SINISTER NEIGHBOURS
• GRAVEYARD
• UNRELIABLE POWER

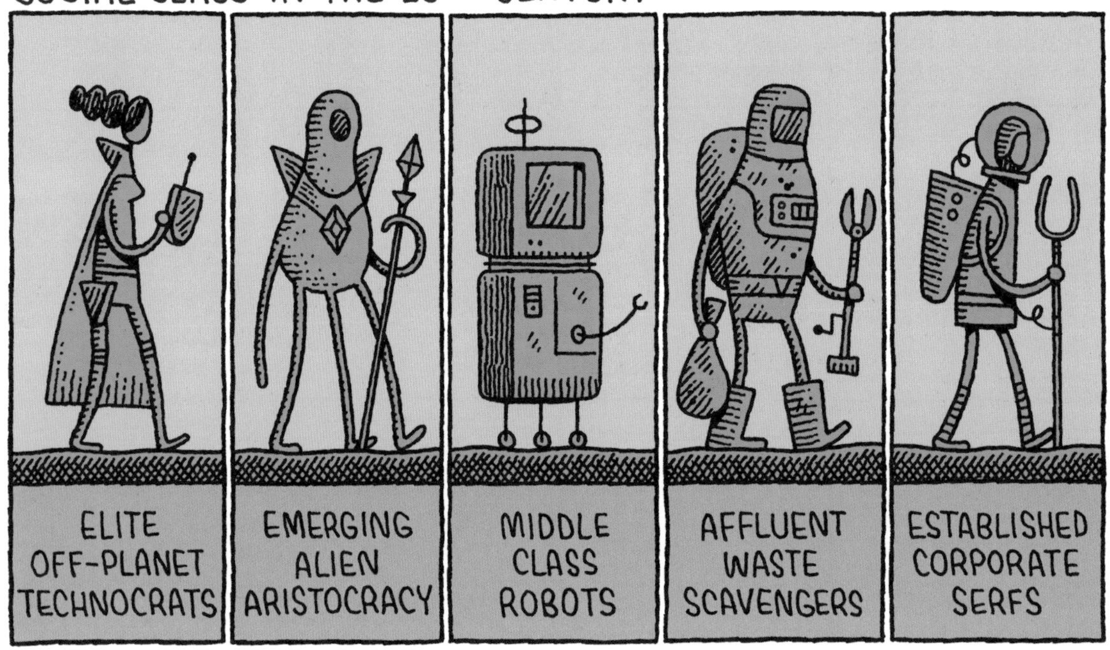
SOCIAL CLASS IN THE 25TH CENTURY
ELITE OFF-PLANET TECHNOCRATS
EMERGING ALIEN ARISTOCRACY
MIDDLE CLASS ROBOTS
AFFLUENT WASTE SCAVENGERS
ESTABLISHED CORPORATE SERFS

FATHER! 'KINGDOM OF IRON' HAS ASKED ME TO MARRY HIM!
WE ARE CLASSICS! NO DAUGHTER OF MINE WILL MARRY A FANTASY NOVEL!
BUT HE IS EPIC AND EXCITING AND I LOVE HIM!
I WON'T HAVE IT! AND BESIDES, I HAVE CHOSEN A HUSBAND FOR YOU...
MEET 'PICKWICK.COM'. HE'S A HUMOROUS MODERN UPDATE OF A CLASSIC!
YO!
NOOOO!

IN BOOKSTORES NOW
THE PENGUIN BOOK OF THE BRITISH SHORT STORY
THE SHORT BOOK OF THE BRITISH PENGUIN STORY
THE STORYBOOK OF THE SHORT, BRITISH PENGUIN
cor blimey!

ENLIGHTENMENT SECTOR
PARTICIPATION SUITE
AWARENESS HABITAT
ORIENTATION NODE
NOURISHMENT HUB
RETAIL COLONY
REST ENVIRONMENTS
CONNECTIVITY SPHERE
THE ANCIENT MONUMENT

HOW TO WRITE A NOVEL
THE ADVANCED GUIDE TO WRITING A NOVEL
FURTHER THOUGHTS ON WRITING A NOVEL
A FEW LAST POINTERS BEFORE YOU START WRITING YOUR NOVEL
SURELY THAT'S ENOUGH ADVICE ABOUT WRITING A NOVEL
I HAVE NOTHING ELSE TO SAY ABOUT WRITING YOUR NOVEL
SERIOUSLY, STOP READING THESE BOOKS AND JUST GET ON WITH WRITING YOUR STUPID NOVEL!
HOW TO WRITE A NOVEL
REVISED AND EXPANDED SECOND EDITION

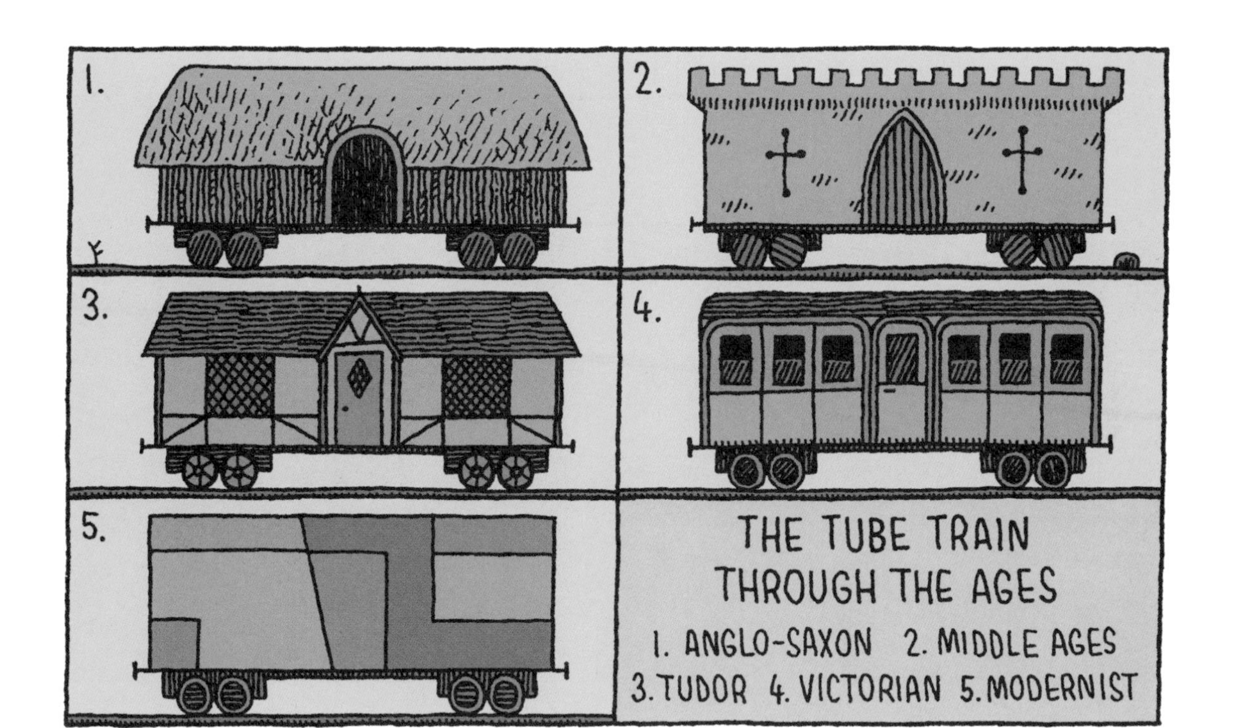
1.
2.
3.
4.
5.
THE TUBE TRAIN
THROUGH THE AGES
1. ANGLO-SAXON 2. MIDDLE AGES
3. TUDOR 4. VICTORIAN 5. MODERNIST

THE REDISCOVERED CLASSIC

HOW THE LITERARY PRIZE WINNER IS CHOSEN
CHAIRMAN
SHORTLISTED NOVEL
REFRESHMENT
JUDGE
LIVELY DEBATE
SPIRITED DISCUSSION

COMMON
MISTAKES
IN
RADIO
INTERVIEWS

NO EYE-CONTACT

TOO COMBATIVE

GIMMICKS

OVER-FAMILIARITY

UNSUITABLE VENUE

QUIZ: HOW DO NOVELS GET TRANSLATED? (TICK ONE BOX)
BLACK MAGIC
TINY ROBOTS
HARD WORK
OSMOSIS

COMMON VILLAINS
EVIL BANKER
NEFARIOUS LAWYER
LOATHSOME INDUSTRIALIST
WICKED SCIENTIST
DEPRAVED ARISTOCRAT
IMMORAL JOURNALIST
LESS COMMON VILLAINS
MONSTROUS FISHMONGER
MALIGNANT BARISTA
FIENDISH LIBRARIAN
DIABOLICAL CERAMICIST
DECEITFUL ZOOKEEPER
TREACHEROUS AUCTIONEER

THIS YEAR'S HOT NEW GENRES
SWORDS, SORCERY AND SELF-HELP
CASTLE OF NEGATIVITY
ECONOMICS PICTURE BOOKS
BROWN RABBIT'S FISCAL RESPONSIBILITY PLAN
POST-APOCALYPTIC SCI-FI POETRY
BINARY SONNETS FOR A PERPETUAL WINTER

FORGOTTEN CHAPTERS OF JANE AUSTEN'S EMMA
THE WITCH'S PROPHECY
BONAPARTE ATTACKS HARTFIELD
EMMA'S WARRIOR TRAINING
WILD WEST ADVENTURE

JANE EYRE UNCOVERS MISTER ROCHESTER'S SECRETS
SO, YOUR MAD WIFE WAS HIDDEN IN THE ATTIC AND YOU PROBABLY HAVE A DAUGHTER WITH A FRENCH DANCER. ANY OTHER SECRETS I SHOULD KNOW?
YES, JANE. A GREAT MANY. I SHALL TELL ALL WHEN WE HAVE BEEN MARRIED FOR ONE YEAR.
I'M NOT FALLING FOR THAT AGAIN. LET'S HEAR THEM NOW.
LATER...
...76. SCARED OF SPIDERS. 77. WAS FAT AS A CHILD. 78. CAN'T RIDE A BICYCLE. 79. VERY HAIRY TOES...
I REALLY MEANT ANY OTHER INTERESTING SECRETS I SHOULD KNOW?
NO.

AT THE BOOK FESTIVAL

NOW AVAILABLE IN THE APP STORE: ANGRY GRAMMARIAN

I'M PRETTY SURE YOU'RE IN THE WRONG PAINTING.

SOME NEW NATURE WORDS

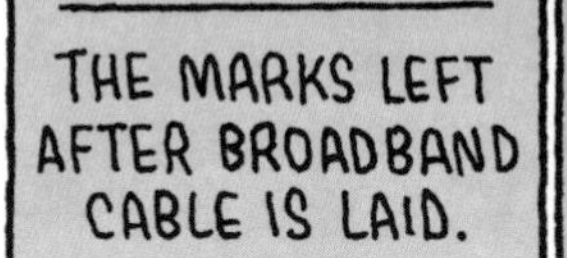

PIPEY-FURROCK
THE MARKS LEFT AFTER BROADBAND CABLE IS LAID.

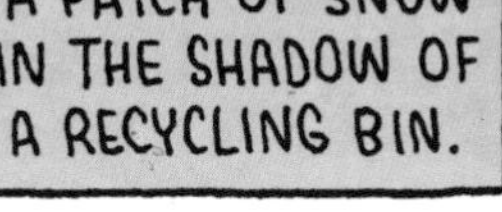

SMOOTLE
A PATCH OF SNOW IN THE SHADOW OF A RECYCLING BIN.

BRUFT
A BIRD'S NEST BUILT ON A CCTV CAMERA.

CROBIE-TINKLER
SUNLIGHT GLINTING OFF A MOBILE PHONE MAST.

I THOUGHT THAT BEING A SCI-FI CHARACTER WOULD BE ALL FLYING CARS, SEXY ROBOTS AND HOLIDAYS ON ALPHA CENTAURI.

MAGICAL ITEMS FOR FANTASY WRITERS
STAFF OF PROTECTION
HELM OF FOCUS
ELIXIR OF COURAGE
AMULET OF ATTRACTION
WARDS OFF SNOOTY CRITICS, PATRONISING REVIEWS AND INTERNET TROLLS
PUTS THE WEARER INTO A WRITING TRANCE WITHIN AN IMPREGNABLE FORCEFIELD
DISPELLS MISGIVINGS, GLOOM, BAD ADVICE AND WRITER'S BLOCK
SUMMONS MAINSTREAM ACCEPTANCE, HOLLYWOOD MONEY AND FRESH COFFEE

THE SENSIBLE CATERPILLAR AND THE STUPID BEETLE
THE SENSIBLE CATERPILLAR WORKED VERY HARD ALL SUMMER, BUILDING A HIGH WALL TO KEEP STRANGERS OUT.
"I'M NOT GOING TO BUILD A WALL" SAID THE STUPID BEETLE, "MAYBE THE STRANGERS WILL BE NICE".
HE REALLY WAS A VERY STUPID BEETLE.
SURE ENOUGH, THE STRANGERS ARRIVED AND THE STUPID BEETLE ATE THEIR STRANGE FOOD AND DANCED THEIR STRANGE DANCES. HE WAS MUCH TOO STUPID TO SEE THAT THEY WERE CHANGING HIS WAY OF LIFE.
THE SENSIBLE CATERPILLAR WAS SAFE AND SOUND BEHIND HIS HIGH WALL. "WHAT A VERY SENSIBLE CATERPILLAR I AM" HE SAID TO HIMSELF.

FEMINIST JAMES BOND

TECHNOLOGY IS MY FRIEND

ADVICE FOR WRITERS #43: BEARDS

1. BEARDS SHOULD BE USED SPARINGLY. TOO MANY BEARDED CHARACTERS WILL CONFUSE THE READER.

2. ESCHEW THE JARGON OF THE BARBERSHOP. BEARDS SHOULD BE DESCRIBED IN SIMPLE, EVERYDAY LANGUAGE.

3. NEVER USE A FULL BEARD WHERE MUTTONCHOPS OR A MOUSTACHE WILL SUFFICE.

OK, BUT ASIDE FROM THE MISCAST LEAD, CLUMSY VOICEOVER, PLOT BUTCHERY, UNSUITABLE SETTING, ILL-JUDGED TONE, HISTORICAL ERRORS, GRATUITOUS NUDITY AND TACKED-ON HAPPY ENDING, ARE YOU PLEASED WITH OUR ADAPTATION OF YOUR NOVEL?

The Sex Scene

ALICE'S
ALLERGY
LIST

SHRINKING.

GROWTH.

BLOATED
FEELING.

FLIGHT,
SUPER-STRENGTH,
X-RAY VISION.

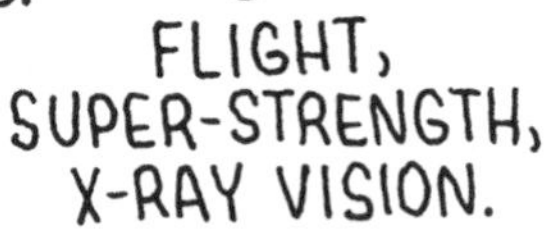
DIZZINESS,
HEADACHE.

NO EFFECT BUT
SHE DOESN'T
REALLY LIKE IT.

SHAPESHIFTING,
HALLUCINATIONS.

ANAPHYLACTIC
SHOCK.

COMMUNICATE
WITH THE DEAD,
SUMMON
ECTOPLASM.

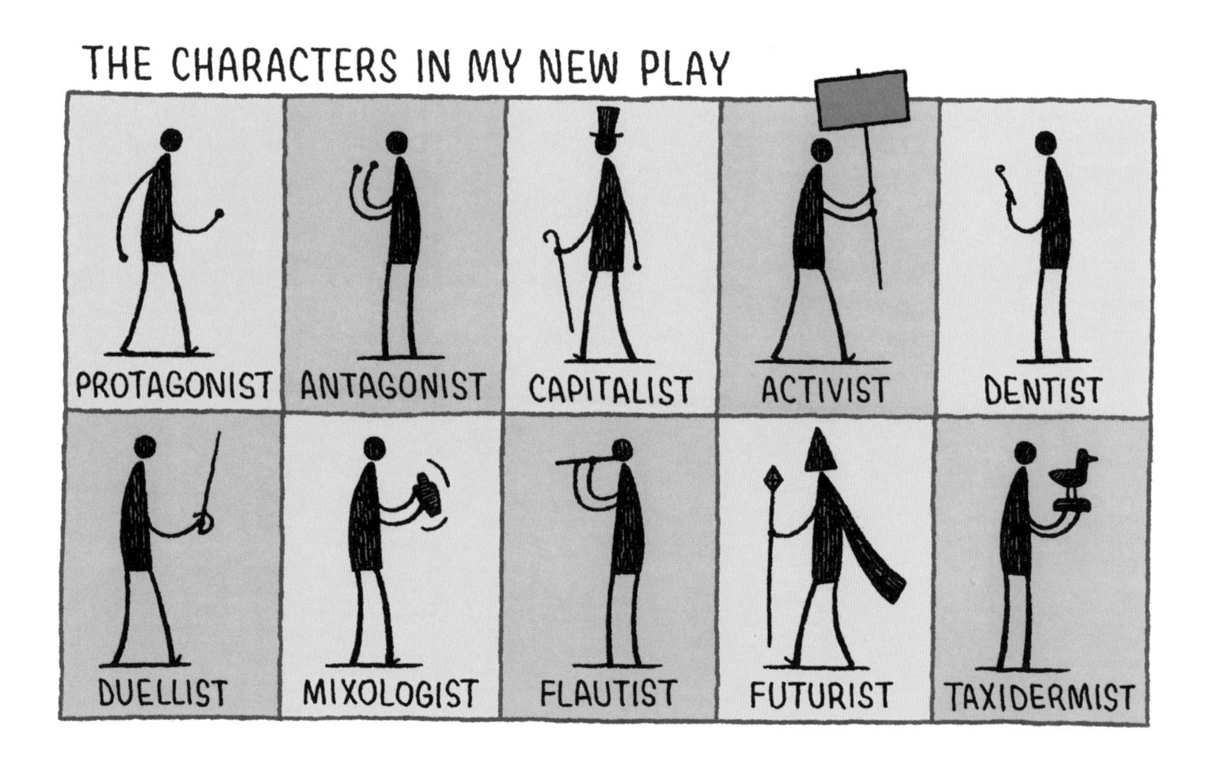
THE CHARACTERS IN MY NEW PLAY
PROTAGONIST
ANTAGONIST
CAPITALIST
ACTIVIST
DENTIST
DUELLIST
MIXOLOGIST
FLAUTIST
FUTURIST
TAXIDERMIST

I AM AN ABJECT FAILURE.
BETTER A FAILED FOUNTAIN THAN A SUCCESSFUL PUDDLE.
I SUPPOSE.
FAILURE PLAYS HIS TRUMPET AT DAWN, BUT SUCCESS RIDES HIS BICYCLE THROUGH THE WOODS AT NIGHT.
WHAT?
FAILURE IS TO SUCCESS AS A THIMBLE IS TO A RHINOCEROS.
PLEASE STOP NOW.

NICCOLÒ MACHIAVELLI'S PLANS FOR THE SUMMER

MON	TUE	WED	THUR	FRI	SAT	SUN
29 PLOT	30 SCHEME	31 CONNIVE	1 BETRAY	2 EXPLOIT	3 CONTROL	4 MISLEAD
5 DENTIST 3PM	6 INTRIGUE	7 COERCE	8 LAST DAY	9 HOLIDAYS! →	10	11
12 ←	13	14 HOLIDAYS	15	16	17	18 →
19 BACK TO WORK	20 DECEIVE	21 COLLUDE	22 MUM'S BIRTHDAY	23 CONSPIRE	24 FINESSE	25 INVEIGLE

OUR TOWN IN LITERATURE: NEW FICTION BY LOCAL AUTHORS

THE TOWN IS A DREARY PRISON FROM WHICH OUR HERO LONGS TO ESCAPE.

AN OUTSIDER MOVES INTO THE TOWN AND UNCOVERS ITS HORRIFYING SECRET.

THE TOWN IS THE BACKDROP TO A SERIES OF HARROWINGLY GRUESOME MURDERS.

TRUE LOVE IS DESTROYED BY THE PETTY SPITEFULNESS OF THE TOWNSPEOPLE.

AN ARMY OF THE UNDEAD ATTACKS THE TOWN AND MASSACRES ITS INHABITANTS.

ELECTRONIC NOSTALGIA

BAD WRITING

A COURSE EXPLORING ALL ASPECTS OF TERRIBLE LITERATURE

BOOK YOUR PLACE NOW AND BECOME THE AWFUL WRITER YOU KNOW YOU CAN BE!

WEEK ONE

FINDING YOUR LOUSY VOICE

WEEK TWO

DEVELOPING YOUR CRUMMY IDEA

WEEK THREE

WRITING APPALLING DIALOGUE

WEEK FOUR

CREATING DREADFUL CHARACTERS

WEEK FIVE

EDITING YOUR PILE OF RUBBISH

WEEK SIX

GETTING YOUR HORRIBLE BOOK PUBLISHED

A MINIATURE MELODRAMA

OUR HERO

A DOCTOR

HIS TRUE LOVE

A LUNATIC ASYLUM

JEALOUS RIVALS

CHAPTER I
OUR TALE BEGINS

CHAPTER II
A FORTUNE!

CHAPTER III
HE FALLS IN LOVE

CHAPTER IV
DEVIOUS PLANS

CHAPTER V
COMMITTED!

CHAPTER VI
DESPAIR?

CHAPTER VII
ESCAPE!

CHAPTER VIII
REVENGE

CHAPTER IX
REUNION

CHAPTER X
A HAPPY ENDING

VILLAGE GREEN 2.0

PURCHASE

VOTED 'BEST ENGLISH VILLAGE SIMULATION APP' 2015

WHAT'S NEW IN VERSION 2.0?

- ENHANCED DETAIL IN PARISH COUNCIL MEETINGS.
- EXPANDED WEATHER MODES: DRIZZLE, LIGHT BREEZE, FLOOD.
- UPDATED CHURCH REPAIR FUNDRAISING OPTIONS.
- NEW CHARACTERS: POSTMISTRESS, B&B INSPECTOR, LANDLORD'S EX-WIFE.
- BUGS FIXED IN PLANNING REGULATIONS MENU.
- ADDED FEATURES: PARKING DISPUTES, SECOND HOMES, BANK HOLIDAYS.
- 'MARKET TOWN' EXPANSION PACK NOW AVAILABLE.

THE 'MORE POETRY FOR CHILDREN' CAMPAIGN PRESENTS

TRANSFORMERS 4: POETIC JUSTICE
THE DECEPTICONS ARE DEFEATED AND IT IS ALL THANKS TO YOU, EMILY DICKINSON.

SEAMUS HEANEY VISITS PEPPA PIG
A SOUL RAMIFYING AND FOREVER SILENT, BEYOND SILENCE LISTENED FOR.

CRIMEFIGHTING WITH SPIDERMAN & GINSBERG
I'LL CATCH THE CROOKS IN MY WEB, THEN YOU BLOW THEIR MINDS WITH A POEM.

CLASSIC LITERATURE WITH ADDED SCIENCE!
SENSE AND SEISMOLOGY
THE OLD CRYSTALLO-GRAPHY SHOP
LADY CHATTERLEY'S LEPIDOPTERIST
THE COLEOPTERIST OF MONTECRISTO
A PORTRAIT OF THE ASTRONOMER AS A YOUNG MAN
TESS OF THE DENDRO-CHRONOLOGISTS
THREE MYCOLOGISTS IN A BOAT

SHE'S A HISTORY PROFESSOR FROM THE FUTURE. SHE SAID TO JUST CARRY ON AS IF SHE'S NOT HERE.

MAJOR STYLES IN TROLL BRIDGE ARCHITECTURE
EARLY ROMANESQUE
GOTHIC REVIVAL
CONCRETE BRUTALISM
GEOMETRIC NEO-FUTURISM

1851: HERMAN MELVILLE CONSIDERS A TITLE FOR HIS NEW NOVEL
THE WHALE?
MOBY-DICK?
OF WHALES AND MEN?
EVERYTHING YOU ALWAYS WANTED TO KNOW ABOUT WHALING BUT WERE AFRAID TO ASK?
AHAB AND MOBY'S EXCELLENT ADVENTURE?
MEN ARE FROM MARS WHALES ARE FROM VENUS?
WHERE'S MOBY?

MILITARY FLAGS FROM THE GRAMMAR WARS OF THE MID-21ST CENTURY

QUEEN'S ENGLISH BRIGADE

PEOPLE'S EMOJI ARMY

CORRECT USAGE STORMTROOPERS

TXT SPK SQDRN

ANGRY PEDANTS MILITIA

PRODUCTIVE TEST WORRIERS

SLANG VANDALS

STYLE GUIDE COMMANDOS

JAMES BOND IS
DRIVING IN HIS
UNDERWATER CAR.

BIP
BIP
BIP
HE GETS A TELEPRINTED
MESSAGE ON HIS
LASER-BEAM WATCH.
A FEMALE 007?

"WHAT A SILLY IDEA!"
THINKS BOND, AS HE
JETPACKS TOWARDS HIS
SPACESHIP, AVOIDING A
METAL-TOOTHED GIANT
AND A RAZOR-SHARP HAT.

221b BAKER STREET...
I HAVE A CASE FOR SHERLOCK HOLMES.
MADAM, I AM SHERLOCK HOLMES.
BUT YOU'RE CLASSIC LITERARY SHERLOCK HOLMES: I WANTED SEXY MODERN SHERLOCK HOLMES.
HE'S OUT ON ANOTHER CASE. IT'S EITHER ME OR CARTOON DOG SHERLOCK HOLMES.
ROWF!
I SUPPOSE YOU'LL HAVE TO DO.
THE GAME IS AFOOT! COME ALONG COMEDY BUMBLING DOCTOR WATSON!

The
MISTER CONSPIRACY THEORY
books...

OUR LOCAL UNDERWORLD
1.
2.
3.
4.
5.
6.
7.
8.
1. ARTISANAL PICKPOCKET
2. EXTRA VIRGIN OLIVE OIL SMUGGLER
3. URBAN EXPLORER
4. RARE-BREED GIANT RAT
5. BESPOKE FOLDING BICYCLE THIEF
6. FERAL BARISTA
7. ORGANIC POISONOUS FUNGI
8. ETHICAL BURGLAR

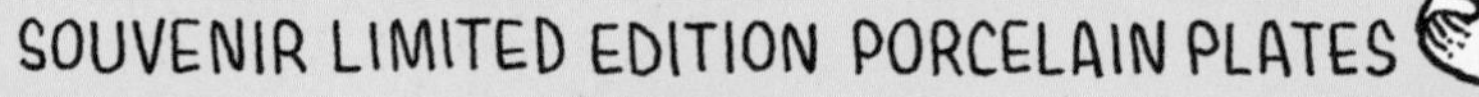

THE MARTIAN INVASION OF 1894
SOUVENIR LIMITED EDITION PORCELAIN PLATES

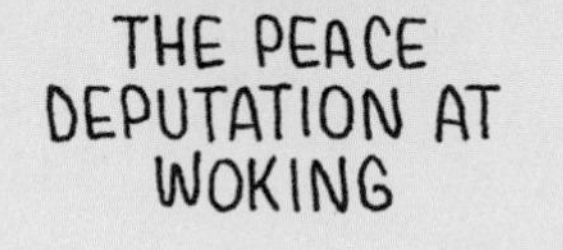

THE DESTRUCTION OF WEYBRIDGE AND SHEPPERTON

THE PEOPLE OF SURREY HARVESTED FOR THEIR BLOOD

HOW DID YOU DECIDE WHICH CANDIDATE TO VOTE FOR?
SCIENTIFIC CALCULATION
MONTHS OF REFLECTION
PURE CHANCE
CELEBRITY ENDORSEMENTS
OCCULT RITUALS

ART
HA HA!
GREEN IDIOT
HA HA!
PURPLE MORON
HA HA!
BLUE PILLOCK
HA HA!
RED ARSE
THIS IS A BLOODY DISGRACE!
ORANGE NITWIT

SAMUEL BECKETT'S SITCOM PITCHES

WAITING FOR KRAMER

TWO MEN, NAMED JERRY AND GEORGE, AWAIT THE ARRIVAL OF A MAN NAMED KRAMER. THEY TALK. TIME PASSES. HE DOESN'T COME. THEY WAIT A BIT LONGER.

NO SEX AND NO CITY

FOUR FEMALE FRIENDS GOSSIP, LAUGH AND FIND WAYS TO DEAL WITH BEING A MODERN WOMAN. THEY ARE ALL BURIED UP TO THEIR NECKS IN SOIL, ON AN OTHERWISE EMPTY SET.

FRASIER'S LAST TAPE

A PSYCHIATRIST AND TALKSHOW HOST SITS ALONE, LISTENING TO RECORDINGS FROM HIS PAST. A NARRATIVE EMERGES, CONCERNING HIS FATHER, BROTHER AND HOUSEKEEPER.

HAVE YOU SEEN MY KINDLE ANYWHERE?

WHO WRITES NOVELS?
59%
WRITERS
11%
GHOST WRITERS
2%
HAUNTED TYPEWRITERS
3.5%
ROBOTS, ALGORITHMS AND COMPUTERS
0.5%
HELPFUL ELVES
4%
SECRET GOVERNMENT AGENCIES
3%
TALENTED ANIMALS
1.5%
VISITING ALIENS
6%
FORGERS, SCAMMERS AND IMPOSTERS
9.5%
NOBODY KNOWS

THE TERRIBLE STORM HAS...

THE MANIFESTO WRITERS GET FEEDBACK FROM THE FOCUS GROUP

PREVIOUSLY UNKNOWN FINAL CHAPTERS OF
'CHARLIE AND THE CHOCOLATE FACTORY'
CHAPTERS 31-35
CHARLIE ATTENDS VARIOUS HEALTH & SAFETY COURSES AND MANAGEMENT SEMINARS.
CHAPTER 36
CHARLIE FENDS OFF AN AGGRESSIVE TAKEOVER BY NESTLÉ.
CHAPTER 37
CHARLIE RENEGOCIATES CONTRACTS WITH THE OOMPA-LOOMPA UNIONS.
CHAPTERS 38-39
CHARLIE DIVERSIFIES INTO NON-CONFECTIONERY AREAS, INCREASING PROFITS 2000%.

OUR JOURNEY WILL BE LONG AND PERILOUS AND NOT ALL WILL SURVIVE:
SOME WILL PERISH ON THE ROAD TO XAGNVRKK,
SOME WILL DIE IN THE AWESOME CLIMAX OF THE THIRD BOOK IN THE TRILOGY
AND SOME WILL MAKE IT ALL THE WAY TO THE END, ONLY TO BE WRITTEN OUT OF THE TV ADAPTATION FOR BEING "TOO LITERARY".

THE END OF THE NOVEL
LET'S GET MARRIED RIGHT AWAY!
YES! LET'S!
CAN YOU DO THAT AFTER WE MARCH ON PARLIAMENT AND STATE OUR RADICAL DEMANDS FOR SOCIETAL CHANGE?
I'M AFRAID NOT: THE WORKERS' UPRISING WAS JUST A SUBPLOT.
WHAT?
THE MAIN STORY IS OUR LOVE BLOSSOMING AMIDST ADVERSITY. SO NOW IT'S TIME FOR A HAPPY ENDING.
WHAT ABOUT US?
BACK TO WORK. SORRY.

THE FUNNY BOOK

THE MAJORITY OF THESE CARTOONS ORIGINALLY APPEARED IN THE GUARDIAN, BUT A FEW WERE COMMISSIONED BY THE NEW YORKER OR THE NEW YORK TIMES. I WOULD LIKE TO THANK SARAH HABERSHON, NICHOLAS WROE, FRANÇOISE MOULY, PEGGY BURNS, TOM DEVLIN, TRACY HURREN, SRUTI ISLAM, JULIA POHL-MIRANDA, FRANCIS BICKMORE, JAMIE BYNG, BILLY KIOSOGLOU, AND MY LOVELY WIFE, JO.

TOM GAULD WAS BORN IN 1976 AND GREW UP IN ABERDEENSHIRE, SCOTLAND. HE IS A CARTOONIST AND ILLUSTRATOR AND HIS WORK IS REGULARLY PUBLISHED IN THE GUARDIAN, THE NEW YORK TIMES, AND NEW SCIENTIST. HIS COMIC BOOKS, 'MOONCOP', 'YOU'RE ALL JUST JEALOUS OF MY JETPACK', AND 'GOLIATH' ARE PUBLISHED BY DRAWN & QUARTERLY. HE LIVES IN LONDON WITH HIS FAMILY.

WWW.TOMGAULD.COM

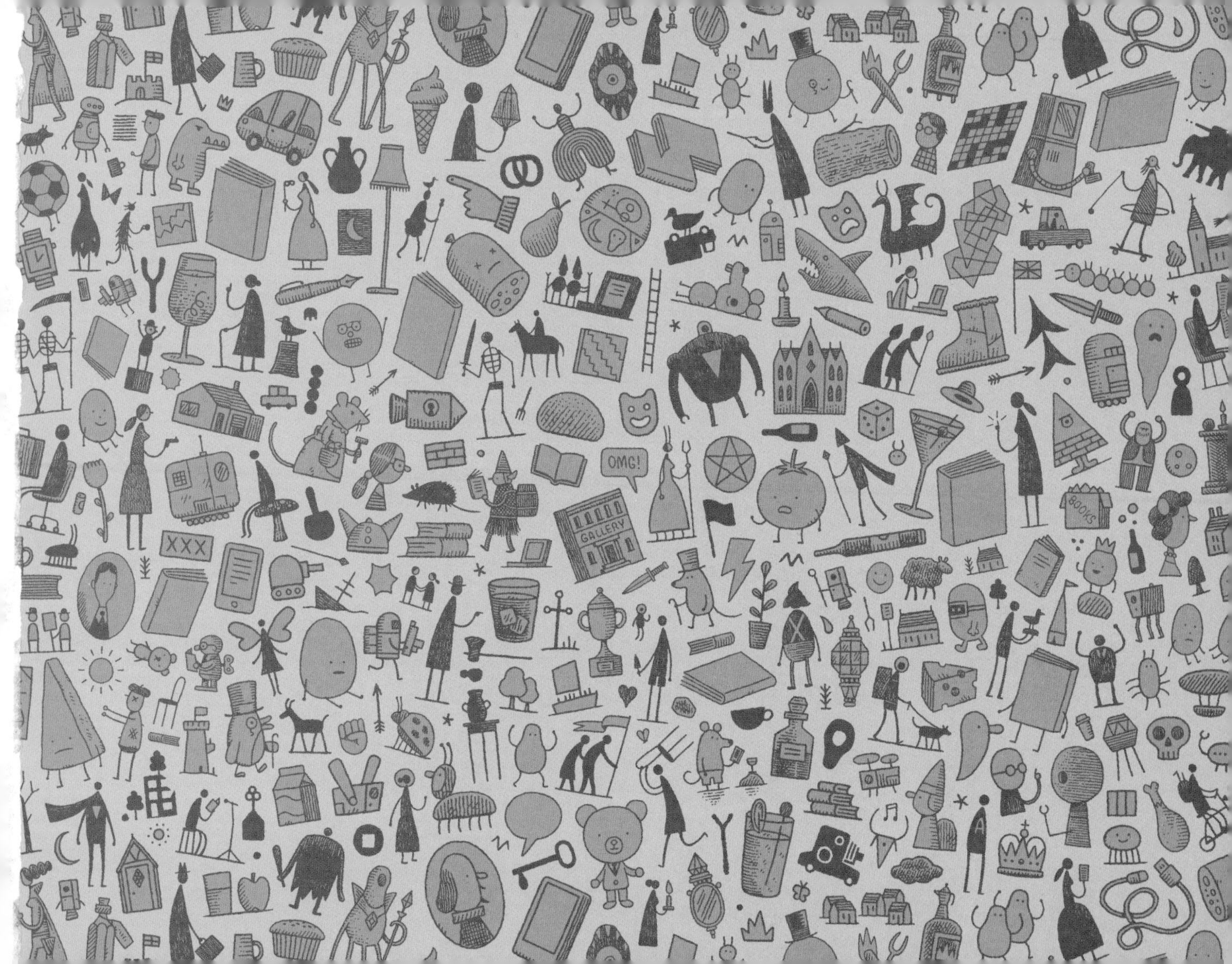
OMG!
GALLERY
XXX
BOOKS

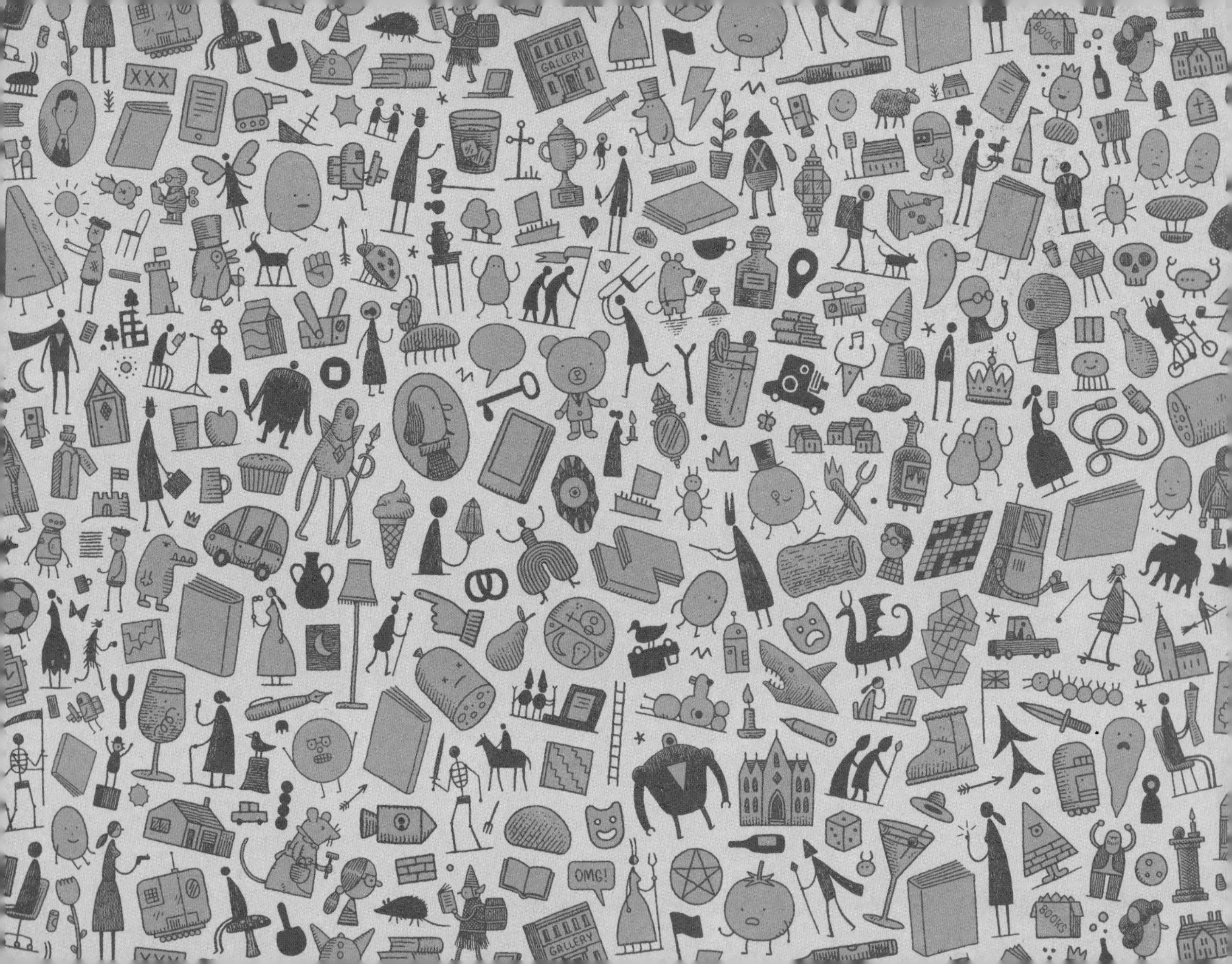

GALLERY
XXX
BOOKS
OMG!